RUDOLF STEINER (1861–1925) called his spiritual philosophy 'anthroposophy', meaning 'wisdom of the human being'. As a highly developed seer, he based his work on direct knowledge and perception of spiritual dimensions. He initiated a modern and universal 'science of spirit', accessible to anyone willing to exercise clear and unprejudiced thinking.

From his spiritual investigations Steiner provided suggestions for the renewal of many activities, including education (both general and special), agriculture, medicine, economics, architecture, science, philosophy, religion and the arts. Today there are thousands of schools, clinics, farms and other organizations involved in practical work based on his principles. His many published works feature his research into the spiritual nature of the human being, the evolution of the world and humanity, and methods of personal development. Steiner wrote some 30 books and delivered over 6,000 lectures across Europe. In 1924 he founded the General Anthroposophical Society, which today has branches throughout the world.

THE KNIGHTS TEMPLAR
The Mystery of the Warrior Monks

RUDOLF STEINER

Compiled and edited by Margaret Jonas

RUDOLF STEINER PRESS

Rudolf Steiner Press
Hillside House, The Square
Forest Row, RH18 5ES

www.rudolfsteinerpress.com

Published by Rudolf Steiner Press 2007
Reprinted 2011

Earlier English publications: See Sources section on p. 161

Originally published in German in various volumes of the GA (*Rudolf Steiner Gesamtausgabe* or Collected Works) by Rudolf Steiner Verlag, Dornach. For further information see Sources, p. 161. This authorized translation is published by permission of the Rudolf Steiner Nachlassverwaltung, Dornach.

All material has been translated or checked against the original German by Christian von Arnim

Photo of Temple Church on page 9 courtesy Tom Raines, *New View* magazine

A catalogue record for this book is available from the British Library

ISBN: 978 185584 179 6

Cover by Andrew Morgan Design featuring detail from Castelo de Tomar (Portugal)
Typeset by DP Photosetting, Neath, West Glamorgan
Printed and bound by Gutenberg Press, Malta

Contents

Introduction

Oh, see the fair chivalry come, the companions of Christ!
White horsemen, who ride on white horses, the Knights of God!
They, for their Lord and their Lover who sacrificed
All, save the sweetness of treading, where He first trod!

Lionel Johnson: *Martyrum Candidatus*

After more than 700 years the name of the Knights Templar
still evokes a strong response. The recent surge of interest
from serious histories to Dan Brown's popular fiction, *The
Da Vinci Code*, shows that some echo is evoked in present day
souls. Were they simply a bunch of loutish crusaders killing
and pillaging and finally being unmasked for their perver-
sions and heretical practices? (Sir Walter Scott's novels
encouraged this view.) Were they simply military monks—an
occupation unappealing to today's mind? Were they a
secretive international group engaged in finance and conspiracy, planning to control the world—a conspiracy fur-
thermore that is still being carried on today by their
descendents in occult brotherhoods? Or were they, as Lionel
Johnson's poem suggests, chivalrous knights relieving the
oppressed and opposing evil, successors to King Arthur's
Round Table? Did they hold the Holy Grail, the Ark of the
Covenant, the Holy Shroud, protect an alleged bloodline of
Jesus Christ, have magical powers, practise alchemy, hide a

fabulous treasure, or make contact with America before Columbus? We can find book after book claiming all these things and more. No fringe history worth its salt today would omit a reference to them; they have become an industry. Serious histories tend to ignore any esoteric connection, whilst popular ones run riot with imagination. It is thanks to Rudolf Steiner's spiritual scientific research that we can begin to get a glimpse of their deeper purpose and meaning, even if we cannot answer all these questions, but first let us look at some historical facts.

By 1100, Crusades to the Holy Land had begun, Jerusalem had been recaptured from the Muslims and was ruled by the Frankish King Baldwin, and the place of Christ's death and resurrection was a popular place for medieval pilgrims. It was, however, dangerous and unstable and thus in 1118 (or 1119 in some sources) an order was founded, allegedly to protect the pilgrims—the Military Order of the Knights of the Temple of Solomon, or Poor Knights of Christ, so called because they were granted the al-Aqsa mosque, believed to be on the site of King Solomon's Temple. There were nine founding knights, with Hugo de Payens becoming the first Grand Master: soldier monks, bound by monastic vows, obliged to repeat the daily monastic offices (except in battle) owing allegiance to none but the Pope, trained in warfare and forbidden to retreat in battle unless the enemy was more than three times their strength. In 1128 at the Council of Troyes, the mighty Cistercian St. Bernard of Clairvaux gave them their Rule, and granted them the right to wear the distinctive white habit—tunic and mantle, with the red equal-armed splayed cross being added in 1147. Their motto was *Non nobis Domine, non nobis, sed Nomini Tuo da Gloriam* (Not for us, Lord, not for us, but in Thy Name the Glory) and their Rule gives in great detail how the monastic vows were expected to be fulfilled:

Obedience

> For with great difficulty will you ever do anything that you wish: for if you wish to be in the land this side of the sea, you will be sent the other side; or if you wish to be in Acre, you will be sent to the land of Tripoli or Antioch, or Armenia; or you will be sent to Apulia, or Sicily, or Lombardy, or France, or Burgundy, or England, or to several other lands where we have houses and possessions. And if you wish to sleep, you will be awoken; and if you sometimes wish to stay awake, you will be ordered to rest in your bed.[1]

Chastity

Not only were sexual relations forbidden, but a monk was not to kiss even his mother or sister, lest he feel temptation. Breeches had to be worn in bed also and a light kept burning in the dormitories to discourage further temptations, though, as we shall see, homosexual activity was later to be levelled against them. Each knight on admission had to wear a red cord around the waist under his tunic to remind him of what had to be overcome.

Poverty

The great wealth amassed by the order did not belong personally to the knights who had to forgo any kind of finery or fancy trimmings to their horses' harness. A Templar seal shows two knights riding one horse, which is usually taken as an example of their poverty. However, another suggestion is that it is more an image of each knight having a helper from the spiritual world.[2]

By 1300, the Order was estimated as having 15,000 men of whom only 1,500 were actual knights, the rest being sergeants, lay brothers and assorted workers. To be a knight one had to be of noble birth and bring a substantial dowry to fund the work of protecting the Holy Land, where a number of castles or fortified preceptories—the name for their 'houses'—were built. In addition to the important task of protecting the Holy Land, preceptories were built in all the main European countries in order to attract suitable fighting men and their wealth. Paris was the chief house in Europe, the site of which is now a small park called the Square of the Temple (Square du Temple). In London the first house was in Holborn, but in 1185 the new London Temple was consecrated with its distinctive round church; the only remaining feature of it which can be seen between the Inner and Middle Temple Inns of Court—between Fleet St and the Thames. Round churches were common—supposedly following the style of the Church of the Holy Sepulchre, the most sacred site in Jerusalem, built on the place of Christ's crucifixion—showing a Byzantine influence, which may also have been present in the forms of worship. However, there are notable Templar churches that are *not* round, such as can be seen at Shipley, and Sompting in Sussex, and round churches that are not necessarily Templar. Much land, including existing churches, was bestowed upon the Order and it is not always easy to discern whether a church was Templar built.

The secrets of church building, the sacred geometry and knowledge of geomancy—the art of where to site according to the flow of earth energy—have been attributed to the Templars, chiefly through surveying remaining sites, but also from the tradition that these secrets were handed on to Masonic guilds and brotherhoods created by the Order, which, it is said, inspired the great medieval cathedrals. There is even a theory that the Templars visited the Americas and brought back silver to fund them.[2a] We can perceive sacred geometry not only in the surviving churches, however, but at sites such as Cressing, Essex, where two magnificent barns remain, displaying skilful joinery in their harmonious proportions, which must have added to their purpose as granaries for keeping the grain fresh. There is a long-standing tradition that certain geometric forms work in this way, for example the Great Pyramid, of which little replicas have been made for this purpose. In the tiled roof of one of the barns, the rune *Ing* (shown thus: ◇) has been picked out—a symbol of fertility to the local Anglo-Danish population. Such practical skills were later to furnish the accusation of magical practices: 'Item, that [these idols] made the trees flower ... the land germinate ...'[3].

Protection of the Holy Land may have been the *raison d'être* for the Order, but two other important functions are sometimes overlooked. The Templars were really the first international bankers. Their widespread organization and integrity as a religious order made it possible for people to deposit their money safely in one country and withdraw it in another, thus preventing theft whilst travelling. Letters of credit—the first cheques—were issued and personal accounts were kept. The Paris Temple had a 'cash desk', and Templars sometimes acted as auditors for other businesses. Usury, the charging of interest on loans, was forbidden by the Church, but this was circumvented by 'bank charges' instead. This highly significant banking activity has been one of the main reasons for hostility towards the Order—bankers are seldom popular, but more especially it has given rise to the conspiracy theory of an international order still existing and controlling the world through finance, see for example Umberto Eco's novel *Foucault's Pendulum*. An interesting theory expressed in a series of history programmes on British TV and now released on DVD entitled *The Knights Templar*, is that after the Order's downfall, some members escaped across the Alps to Switzerland and were instrumental in setting up the Swiss cantons as administrative regions. The secretive Swiss financial institutions would be obvious heirs also.

Connected to this function is their other important contribution to the medieval economy in general. They put the land they held to the fullest use in establishing farms, vineyards, mills, mines and all kinds of industry, crafts and trade, thus providing work for local people and a steady income from rent. Markets were set up in small towns and, in villages, land was cleared, drained, fenced, stocked and generally well maintained. Thus the Order held a lot of local control often over and above other landowners, whether religious or secular, and its exemption from taxation increased the discontent felt by some.

As time went on, criticism of the Order grew on account of its wealth and power and alleged arrogance. But then, disturbingly, other rumours began to circulate, horrifying to the medieval mind: secret rituals, which involved denying or spitting upon the Cross, worshipping idols or black cats, homosexual activity not only being tolerated but encouraged, obscene kisses—*Beware the kiss of the Templars* came to be a smutty joke. And the further accusation of treason was made—alliances with the Saracen enemy. In the Holy Land or *Outremer,* the situation had changed. Saladin recaptured Jerusalem in 1187 and a Christian army did not re-enter until 1917 under General Allenby. For another century the Order remained as a strong influence, still holding several castles, but in 1291 the city of Acre (Acco) fell to the Muslims and the Order was obliged to withdraw altogether, setting up an Eastern presence on Cyprus. Why then should it continue to exist at all, asked some, or could it not be merged with the fellow Order of Knights Hospitallers? It might have carried on in some form for years had it not been for the greed of the King of France, Philip the Fair, whose nature belied his name, for he was cold, ruthless and opportunistic. He was possessed by an inordinate lust for gold and had already confiscated the wealth of the Jews and Lombards and had debased the gold coinage. Steiner suggests moreover, that he may have been initiated in a previous lifetime into the bloodthirsty and black magical Mexican mysteries, tearing the hearts from living victims.[4] In fact after his death, when his heart was embalmed and sent to the monastery of Poissy, it was said to be tiny and shrivelled. He also had imperial expansionist dreams and tried to join the Order but was rejected. Incensed, he was determined to acquire its wealth. He first manipulated the Papacy to get his own 'puppet',

Clement V, installed on French soil at Avignon. He infil-
trated the Order via his agents and persuaded the Pope that
the Templars must be disbanded and brought to trial for
heresy, sodomy and blasphemy. He struck at dawn on Friday
13th October 1307 with an operation worthy of a twentieth
century secret police organization. Orders had been secretly
issued beforehand—all Templars that could be found were
arrested in one swoop.

It was less easy to persuade his fellow monarchs to do
likewise—arrests and torture of the Templars varied from
country to country. In England, Edward II forbade torture
but later confiscated the Order's property for himself,
whilst Portugal, Majorca and Aragon refused to believe the
accusations and allowed the Order to continue in different
forms. In France, however, trials were prepared and confessions produced under tortures that were as horrible as
anything devised today. Many Knights subsequently
recanted so that, in 1310, 54 were burned and the Order
was formally dissolved in 1312. On 18 March 1314 the last
Grand Master, Jacques de Molay, and Geoffroi de
Charney, were burned at the stake near the Pont Neuf on
the Île de la Cité. Before he died, Jacques de Molay called
upon Philip and Pope Clement to appear before God—and
both were dead within a year. In Scotland there were no
arrests and many knights joined the campaigns of Bruce
and Wallace against the English. In most countries there
was some form of admonition however; the lands and
properties passed to the Order of Hospitallers, and former
Templars were obliged to join other religious orders, still
being bound by their monastic vows. Historians vary in

Painted medieval wooden panel from the Templecombe Church, Somerset

The Temple Church, London

their judgement, but tend to suppose there was some truth in the accusations, for how else could such a mighty, brave and powerful organization be brought down?

Let us now see what the spiritual aspect reveals. Steiner spoke about the Templars in several places and also wove them into the medieval scenes in his second Mystery Drama *The Soul's Probation* (see note 7 in Sources) where they are in conflict with the local Dominicans. As if trying to set the record straight, he spoke unreservedly of their spiritual dedication. Their blood, he said, belonged to Christ: '. . . each one of them knew this. Every moment of their life was to be filled with the perpetual consciousness of how in their own soul there dwelt—in the words of St. Paul—not I, but Christ in me'.[5]

The human blood system carries both our ego-consciousness and also the rhythms of our etheric—our life—forces. Repeated prayer and meditation both have a powerful effect and enable the blood to 'resonate' with Christ. (The Russian Orthodox Church knows this with the practice of the 'Jesus Prayer'). When not in battle, the Templars recited the daily offices and heard mass (they had their own chaplains), they were permeated with the effects of such rituals. So intense was their inward penetration that many attained a truly Christian initiation—this is too lengthy to enlarge upon here: but see endnote.[6] They were, moreover, part of the esoteric Christian stream of St John, which includes the Manichaeans,[6a] the Grail, and the Rosicrucians. Here the mystery of transformation of physical substance by the power of Christ's blood when it fell to the earth is recognized, and the future redemption of evil is a distant goal. In an early lecture,[7] Steiner described the Templars as actually being initiated by the Grail itself. How might we understand this? In initiation the etheric body (the body of our life forces) is to some extent loosened from the physical body, and this is what was said to have happened to those who witnessed Christ's death on Good Friday. One aspect of the Grail legends is that Christ's blood, which had unsullied etheric (life) forces, was carried in human hearts (a chalice or cup is an image for the heart) so that in Wolfram von Eschenbach's *Parzival*[23], the Templars are known as the Guardians of the Grail.[8] That the Templars were an inspiration for *Parzival* (written down during their time) is confirmed by Steiner.[9] The transformation of one's ether body, which includes what Steiner called 'the etherization of the blood', has an effect not only on the person in question, but rays out into the whole world owing to the ether body's connection to the cosmos. It is this aspect of the Grail—blood mystery rather than guardianship of a physical cup—that is significant.

Another perhaps more surprising aspect of the Templars' spiritual life was their devotion to the divine feminine in the person of the Virgin Mary and also possibly Mary Magdalene. There is not much obvious evidence of this save that their churches were almost always dedicated to 'Our Lady'. It was a feeling they would have had for the manifestation of heavenly wisdom as *Sophia*, a Gnostic-inspired belief. In the old Egyptian mysteries she was known as Isis, and it has been suggested that the Templars knew this (though not consciously) from former incarnations.[2] Moreover, esoteric Freemasonry, which is connected to the Order, takes its founding from the time just after Christ, when the rite of

Misraim was founded by Ormus, a priest of Isis, and St Mark in Alexandria,[10] and the later Scottish Rite was said to have arisen from the Templars surviving in Scotland. Clearly the extreme avoidance of female company was unbalanced (say, in comparison with the Cathars, also part of this broader esoteric stream), and one can only wonder at what was being prepared in their souls.

To what extent their beliefs were 'heretical', is hard to say. They did not found a separate Church for instance. But they were encouraged to seek out those who had been excommunicated by the Church as possible recruits, an unusual command. There were many early Christian beliefs and practices that were later deemed heretical, conveniently labelled Gnostic, though there was no single gnostic school of thought. Teachings came from Egypt, from the Greek mysteries and from esoteric Jewish groups such as the Essenes. One idea that appeared in different guises was that Jesus did not really die on the cross. Many gnostic believers were aware that the divine being of Christ had entered into the man Jesus at the Baptism, and could not reconcile this with the idea of Christ's death. A God could not die, they thought. He must have withdrawn *before* the death, or someone else was crucified in his place—there were various theories with the result that the cross was not necessarily venerated in the way the Church taught. It was inconceivable to people imbued with the gnostic understanding of a God that descended from the spiritual spheres, that such a God should have chosen to experience death as a human being. Many Manichaeans, of whose stream the Templars were a part, in particular held these beliefs. In the Middle East, the

Templars came into contact with these various teachings which had often been kept alive by small groups or which were more or less 'non-Christian'. It would be hardly surprising therefore if these did not come to influence their practices. Perhaps they did not fully grasp the mystery of Christ's incarnation. After all, how many people do today? They also had a special reverence for John the Baptist, which has even led to the suggestion that they could not really have been Christian. He was for them the *Water Bearer*, the precursor of the Age of Aquarius to come, the preparer (by water) of the future Christian way of Baptism by Fire, the time of true brotherhood, when through Christ the meaning of the Temple will be renewed.[11]

Steiner confirmed in conversation that there was a secret order within the Templars. It was this that was one of the issues—at the trials there were confessions about the holding of secret 'chapters', which only certain brothers could attend. Under torture the accused described how they were received into these—they were required to spit upon or defile the cross, to strip naked and receive kisses on the mouth, the navel and the genitals, to venerate a bearded 'head' or 'idol'. What could this mean? Steiner describes how the Templars went through a kind of 'denial of the cross', a ritual re-enactment of Peter's denial of Christ, in order to understand it later, to pass through the stages of the four elements on the arms of a cross symbolising the ego, astral, etheric and physical bodies. The seven-stage ceremony then culminated in their being shown an image of the divine Father creator.[11] One can see how this became distorted when revealed under torture. At the site of the former preceptory of Templecombe in Somerset, a medieval wooden panel was found which shows the head of a man, bearded and with a remarkably expressive countenance (see p. 9). It may be a representation of Christ—or it could be the image that was venerated in the rituals. The figure on the Turin shroud may also have been used in this way. The image could appear 'beautiful' or 'luminous' or terrible, like a bleeding head on a platter. At the trials, the head or idol was sometimes named as *Baphomet*. There is much speculation about the meaning of this name. Idries Shah claims it is known in Sufism as the 'Head of Wisdom'. The thirteenth century esoteric Jewish work, the *Zohar*, also refers to the divine creator revealing himself as a mighty bearded head, with a lower shadow-like reflection or counterpart. A detailed account is not possible here, but it suggests the Knights could have had an experience at the threshold of the spiritual world, which could manifest as one of either grandeur or of terror as the pupil is confronted by his own, darker, side. The Templars had contact with these mystical non-Christian beliefs in the Middle East, for on the whole they practised diplomacy rather than persecution, and made positive contacts with the indigenous population of Muslims, Jews and others, thus incurring the accusation of treachery. What of the so-called obscene kisses? One suggestion is that they were given to acknowledge the chakra system in the human subtle-energy bodies, and what had to be overcome in the lower chakra region in particular. A transmission of energy called *baraka*, passing the breath from a master to a pupil was an Eastern practice that may have been followed also—if these 'kisses' happened at all. Why then did the knights apparently confess to so many deeds that horrified their accusers?

Steiner speaks of this in connection with the effect of torture. Under great physical and mental pain, they came to believe that they had actually committed actions which they had striven to overcome in themselves.[12] The confessions were largely false. In one of his lectures, Steiner states that this was due to the influence of certain 'adversary powers' and revealed more about these, although the subject can only be touched upon here. In speaking about the Apocalypse, the Book of Revelation of St John, he refers to one of the most powerful adversary forces, the anti-Christ, Sorat, the Sun Demon, in connection with the rhythm of 666. Twice this figure is 1332, a little after the Templars' downfall, but it is clear from history that Sorat's influence can extend both before and after a specific date. Steiner stated that it was none other than the spirits belonging to this being who entered into the Templars under torture and caused them to vilify themselves.[13] This is perhaps why Steiner said in response to a question from an early Waldorf teacher that Baphomet was an ahrimanic entity.[13a]

But were all the confessions entirely false or did they simply appear confused and were misunderstood? For centuries this has occupied anyone interested in the Templars. Here and there documents have appeared which claim to be the 'secret statutes' of the inner order, which were found in the Vatican archives and passed on by Masonic Lodges. They were published in a French history some years ago.[14] It is very difficult to say whether they are true, or complete forgeries or somewhere in between. I am inclined to think there is some truth in them but with probable later embellishments. The practices may also have evolved gradually, or could include aberrations in some form, which were not practised by the whole Brotherhood. They speak of two grades with the inner order: the *elect* and the *consoled*. Other Christian movements such as the Manichaeans and Cathars also had two 'grades' or levels. There is a distinct anticlerical tone, indeed a hatred with regard to the Roman Church, and an exhortation to meet with similarly-minded men of other faiths, such as Muslims and Jews, as well as with Cathars and Bulgars. The reception included a trampling and spitting upon the cross because 'the Son was not born, nor died, nor was crucified or resurrected'[14], at the same time 'Jesus' must be revered and all people are 'One' in the true Christ the Lord. Kisses were received by the neophyte as indicated earlier, but clearly not intended to be erotic—this is usually misunderstood today. A dying brother should only confess to an 'Elect'. The veneration of the 'head' or 'Baphomet' was the final stage of initiation as a 'Consoled' brother, known as the 'Baptism of Fire'. The prayer from St John, Chapter 17, and that from the beginning of the Koran, were both read aloud. Altogether they are a strange mixture of statements that could have been taken from the trials yet woven with scriptural references with undoubted reverence, and show an attempt ahead of its time to encourage greater freedom of action and thinking, of mixing with and respecting people of other beliefs with a sense of Oneness, of studying the esoteric and not fearing inner experiences—in short all that was actively frowned upon by the Roman Church. It is difficult to convey the unusual mood and tone of this document, although it could also be a complete fabrication.

This has been an attempt to throw light on the Templars'

outer, or exoteric, history as well as some of their more unusual practices and beliefs. No doubt they will continue to be a subject for occult and political conspiracies and other mysteries both factual and fictitious. They will continue to arouse hatred, fear or admiration and reverence. Their fruits remain in the spiritual world as a source of inspiration for later generations, and their reincarnated souls are often thought to be active in promoting new forms of social life such as a threefold system based on liberty, equality and fraternity, which was premature and went tragically astray in the French Revolution. The guillotining of Louis XVI and Marie Antoinette were felt by some to be an avenging of an Order destroyed by an earlier French king. In a world so ravaged by religious fanaticism, it may be harder for us today to appreciate the value of a movement that sought to protect what were considered to be the most holy places. But it also tried to draw together the different strands of belief of Jew, Muslim and Christian in the spirit of Parsifal who cannot become the next Grail King until he has led his Muslim half-brother Feirefiz to the Grail Castle. In their own way the Templars lived out the Manichaean ideal and penetrated darkness in order to release some light, a dangerous and ultimately destructive path for them, but one that nevertheless reaped a spiritual harvest. They live on in legends such as the one from Gavarnie, in the Pyrenees, which still produces a frisson: on the eve of the anniversary of the Order's downfall, a ghostly figure wearing Templar apparel rides into the local cemetery and calls three times: 'Who will defend the Holy Temple, who will liberate the Sepulchre of the Lord'? Then seven heads belonging to seven martyred

Knights reply three times: 'No one, no one, the Temple is destroyed'![15] This legend was included by the composer Sir John Tavener in his magnificent eight-hour work *The Veil of the Temple*, first performed in 2003 in London's Temple Church, and it shows they still can be a force which inspires souls today. Tavener, moreover, has the choir conclude almost at the end with: 'Who will defend the Holy Temple? Who will deliver the Tomb of Christ?' And the response: 'No, no, no, the Temple is *not* destroyed forever'.

Margaret Jonas

1. Pope Nicholas I and the spiritual life of Europe

1 October 1922

This lecture sets the scene, the background to the Crusades and what inspired them. In 1270, the date cited for their end, Acre (Acco) fell and the Templars—and a Christian presence—were finally driven out of the Holy Land. In the twenty-first century we mostly feel uncomfortable about these Crusades and the inability to show respect for other faiths. (Incidentally, the Templars in the Near East were accused of showing too much respect for Islam) but we can perhaps begin to appreciate better the motivation for pursuing them. Why is the material on Pope Nicholas I[16] important? A highly significant karmic background is revealed here.

Steiner discusses the importance of the Grail stream that spread across from the Near East into western and northern Europe. Though he does not mention it here, behind this there hovered the individuality of Mani, the founder of the earlier Manichaean stream of Christianity, to which the Templars were connected[6a]. Mani reincarnated into the historical personality represented by Parsifal. As mentioned in the Introduction, the Templars were also Knights of the Grail. By the time of Pope Nicholas, Manichaeism itself had reached eastern Europe, and spread into regions that would later belong to the eastern Orthodox churches in the beliefs of the Paulicians for example. It is hard for us to appreciate exactly why Nicholas felt these separations had to take place, and why the deadening effect of 'dogma' was held so forcibly, but Rudolf Steiner endeavours to tease this out. Further light on the deep significance of the Pope's deed for the twentieth century and beyond is shed in the book Light for the New

Millenium,[17] concerning the role of Count Helmuth von Moltke— revealed through Steiner's research as the reincarnated Nicholas I.

In the last few lectures we have been studying impulses of far-reaching influence in the historical evolution of humanity— great impulses which are like the tracks of stars across history, illuminating our understanding of particular events. Knowledge of an epoch in history can only be external and superficial if the underlying impulses are not perceived and understood. For these impulses are real powers; they work for the most part, and they work most powerfully, through the unconscious forces of the soul; what transpires outwardly and in full consciousness is only to be perceived in the right light when its origin can be traced back to them.

Let us consider an event or, more precisely, a series of events well known to history and of profound significance in the whole life of the West during the Middle Ages—a series of events which, in the outer world, ended in a comparatively short time after about a century or a century and a half. But their effects did not end there and, to those able to understand the deeper currents in the flow of world history, have continued to the present day. I refer to the Crusades which began in the eleventh century—1096 is the year usually assigned—and as a series of outer events continued until the year usually given as 1270. But we find that even external history mentions all kinds of enterprises and institutions which developed out of the Crusades.

We hear, for example, of the Templar Knights, who first assumed their real significance in outer life during the time of the Crusades. We hear, too, of orders like that of the Knights of St John[18] later the Knights of Malta, and others. Things that were inaugurated by these communities of secular and spiritual life, and thus sprang from the spirit pervading the Crusades, subsequently developed in such a way that, while their provenance in the Crusading spirit was less and less remarked, their effects and influences were clearly present in the life of the West.

Thinking, to begin with, of the external course of history, we know how the Crusades originated. Needs of the soul led adherents of Christianity in the West to believe that pilgrimages to Palestine would imbue their Christian impulses with fresh vigour; but they encountered obstacles because Palestine and Jerusalem had fallen into the hands of a people of very alien character, namely the Turks. The maltreatment inflicted by the Turks upon these pilgrims to Jerusalem had provoked an outcry all over Europe and from this was born the mood and spirit which gave rise to the Crusades—a mood which had been present for a long time, although in a different form. We see how people gave vent to this mood by demanding the liberation of the holy places of the West, the holy places of Christendom, from Turkish oppression.

We hear how Peter of Amiens,[19] himself a victim of this oppression, travelled through western Europe as a pilgrim and by his fervent preaching won over many hearts to the project of liberating Jerusalem from the Turks. We know too that, to begin with, this led to no result. But soon a whole number of knights in the West, gathering together under the leadership of Godfrey of Bouillon[20] in the first real Crusade, succeeded in liberating Jerusalem, for a time at least, from the Turks.

The course of these events requires only brief mention, for the story is familiar enough in history. The really important thing is to study with insight and understanding what was working more or less unconsciously through human souls in such a way that again and again, and for a long period of time, numbers of men, in most cases with extraordinary devotion and valour, set out upon these journeys to the East, these seven Crusades under the leadership of the most distinguished princes of the West. The real question is this: from where did that first fiery enthusiasm which swept across Europe, especially at the beginning of the Crusades, come? Once the ball had been set rolling—if I can put it like that—interests of a different sort crept in from the fourth Crusade onwards. There were European princes who went to the East with quite other motives, to enhance their power, their prestige and the like. Nevertheless, the beginning of the Crusades is an historical event of prime importance. We cannot fail to be impressed by the spectacle of this mighty force prompting a large part of European humanity to an undertaking linked, as they felt, with the most sacred concerns of the heart. People felt that these sacred concerns were vitally connected with the liberation of Jerusalem from the Turks, in order that Christians in Europe wanting to visit the grave of the redeemer might find their ways cleared.

The dry, prosaic accounts of the historical facts which can be read in books do not, as a rule, convey any real impression of the fire of enthusiasm that flamed up in Europe when that noble company of knights set out on the first Crusade, nor of the rekindling of this enthusiasm by the ardour of men like Bernard of Clairvaux[21] and others. There is an awe-inspiring grandeur about the birth of the Crusades and we cannot help asking ourselves: what impulses were working in the hearts and souls of Europeans at that time—what were the impulses out of which sprang the spirit of the Crusades?

These impulses can only be rightly understood if we trace their development back through the centuries. A pivotal point in history, and one which throws a flood of light upon subsequent happenings of incisive importance in Europe, is the reign of Pope Nicholas I,[16] approximately in the middle of the ninth century, between the years 858 and 867. Before his inner eye, Nicholas I perceived three streams of spiritual life—three streams confronting him like great question marks of civilization. He saw the one stream moving as it were in spiritual heights across from Asia into Europe. In this stream certain conceptions innate in oriental religion were making their way in a much modified and changed form across southern Europe and northern Africa, to Spain, France, the British Isles and especially to Ireland. In view of what I will say later, I will call this the first stream. Originating in the Arab regions of Asia, it flows across Greece and Italy but also across Africa into Spain and then upwards through the West. But its influence also rays out, in different forms, towards other parts of Europe.

Little is said of this stream in the tale told to us as history. We will speak today only of two characteristic features of this stream—which was immeasurably deep in content. One of these is what may be called the esoteric conception of the

Mystery of Golgotha. I have often spoken to you of the conception of the Mystery of Golgotha held by those in whom vestiges of the ancient, pre-Christian initiation knowledge survived. There is an indication of this in the Bible itself—in the coming of the three Magi or Kings from the East. With their knowledge of the secrets of the stars they foresaw the approaching Christ event and set out in search of it. Pre-eminently, therefore, the three Magi are examples of men concerned less with the earthly personality of Jesus of Nazareth than with the all-important fact that a spiritual being had descended from worlds of spirit and soul, that Christ had come to dwell in the body of Jesus of Nazareth and would impart a mighty impulse to the further evolution of the earth. These men viewed the event of Golgotha from a wholly supersensory standpoint. Vision of the supersensory truth was possible to men in whom the ancient principles of initiation had been kept alive, for comprehension of this supersensory event, unintelligible in the natural and historical life of the earth, could be achieved with the help of this ancient initiation knowledge.

But it became more and more difficult to keep alive these ancient principles of initiation and therefore more and more impossible to find appropriate language in which to convey how Christ had come down from supersensory worlds, had passed through the Mystery of Golgotha, and how his power continues to work through all the subsequent evolutions of the earth. People simply had no means of shaping their concepts and ideas in such a way that they could find words to convey what had actually come to pass through Christ and through the Mystery of Golgotha.

And so in order to clothe this mystery in words, people were forced more and more to pictorial forms of presentation. One such is the story of the Holy Grail, of the precious cup which is said, on the one hand, to be the cup with which Christ Jesus had partaken of the Last Supper with his apostles, and, on the other, the cup in which the Roman soldier at the foot of the cross caught the blood flowing from the redeemer. This cup was then carried by angels—and here is the touch of the supersensory, tendered in faltering words, for what the old initiates could have conveyed in clear concepts could now only be conveyed by pictures—this cup was carried by angels to Mont Salvat in Spain and received there by the noble king Titurel;[22] he built a temple for the chalice and there dwelt the Knights of the Holy Grail, keeping watch and ward over the treasure that shields the impulse flowing onwards from the Mystery of Golgotha.

And so we have there a deeply esoteric stream, passing over into a mystery. On the one side we perceive the influence of this deeply esoteric stream in the founding of academies in Asia, where human beings studied the ancient Greek philosopher Aristotle, endeavouring to understand the event of Golgotha with the aid of Aristotelian concepts. Later on, in European civilization, we see attempts made in such a poem as *Perceval/Parzifal*[23] to convey the living content of this esoteric stream in pictures. We see this same living content shimmering through the teachings that arose especially in the schools of Ireland. We see too how the best elements of Arabian wisdom flowed into this stream but how, at the same time, Arabian thought introduced an alien element, coarsened and corrupted in Asia by Turkish influence.

We will speak later, when we have considered the other streams, of the character imparted to this first stream by the Arabian influence and by its advance from the East towards the West. To indicate the fundamental character of this stream, one would be obliged to say: those who were connected in any real way with this stream of spiritual life held the view that the one and only way of salvation—and an echo of this is heard in Wolfram von Eschenbach's *Parzifal*—lay in rising above the sensory and material world into the supersensory, in having at any rate some vision of the supersensory worlds, in letting human beings share in the life of the supersensory worlds, in bringing home to them that their souls belonged to a stream not immediately to be perceived by senses directed to terrestrial events.

The feeling characterizing this gaze upward into supersensory, super-earthly regions was that, in order to be a full human being, people must belong to worlds transcending material existence, worlds whose happenings are hidden from the outward eye as were the deeds of the Knights of the Grail. The mystery implicit in this stream was felt to be somehow imperceptible to the physical eyes.

This, then, was the first stream, barely felt and yet looked at suspiciously in Rome at the time of Pope Nicholas I in the ninth century. The whole tendency in Rome was to regard it as a detrimental influence and one to which it would be harmful for Western humanity to yield. In the religious and intellectual life of Europe there must be nothing of the esoteric, nor anything even faintly deriving from the esoteric, such was the attitude.

This was the first and certainly the most overwhelming

issue to face Nicholas I, for he also discerned the grandeur of this stream of spiritual life. Although much dimmed since the third or fourth century (when a society had actually been founded in Italy for the extermination of all paths to spiritual knowledge) its radiance still shone by way of many hidden openings into the hearts of human beings, revealing itself now here, now there. What broke through in this way into the experience of human beings, often from mysterious strata underlying the progress of history, was denounced as heresy. The feeling also prevailed that the esotericism still faintly glimmering in this stream could no longer find its way into those concepts which, in the culture of Latin Rome, had departed more and more from the inwardness of Greek thought with its oriental colouring and had adopted the forms of Roman rhetoric—in other words, had become formal and exoteric. Yet on the other hand, among individuals and communities denounced as heretical sects, this stream flashed into life with tremendous power.

The second question of world history before the soul of Nicholas I was this. All the knowledge gathered up to that point by the Catholic Church forced him to the conclusion that the Europeans of the West were incapable of bearing the great spiritual tension that is evoked in the souls of human beings if they are to scale the heights of spiritual, esoteric understanding. A great uncertainty weighed upon the soul of Nicholas I. What will happen if too much of this esoteric spiritual stream makes its way into the souls of the people of Europe?

In the East itself, greater and greater confusion had crept into what had once been the esoteric content of this stream. It was over in far-off Ireland that it maintained its purest form and for some time there were Schools in Ireland where the holy secrets were preserved in great purity. But—so pondered Nicholas I—this is useless for the people of Europe. Nicholas I was, in reality, only repeating the view previously held by Boniface[24] in a somewhat different form, namely that owing to their intrinsic character the people of Europe were not adapted for the inflow of spiritual life into their souls. And so the strange position arose that in the East the real, esoteric substance died away. Human beings living in the East and also in the east of Europe, in the regions of present-day Russia, could make no contact in their souls with this esoteric substance. But over in the East, purely in the form of feelings, and in so far as these feelings had not been utterly exterminated by the gradual advance of the Turanian peoples—the Turks—over in the East human beings had a dim feeling that the sublimely esoteric, which cannot be comprehended by the dawning intellect, flows in cult and ritual; but only when the cult has at the same time an actual centre in the outer world, a geographical centre.

And so in the east of Europe, while the esoteric, spiritual reality was forgotten, human beings turned to cult and ritual, clinging with greatest intensity of feeling to what they held to be the very heart and core of the cult: the grave of the redeemer. Close to the grave of the redeemer in Jerusalem was the place where he had celebrated the Last Supper with his apostles, that Eucharistic meal which in metamorphosis became the death on Golgotha, was consummated by this death and then lived on—in the central rite, but also in the whole ritual—in the Mass.

In their estrangement, because they failed to reach an esoteric understanding of the spiritual reality, human beings gave their hearts to cult and ritual, and to that with which the cult was outwardly connected: the grave of the redeemer and the holy places in Jerusalem. Pilgrimage to Jerusalem came to be regarded as crowning all the solemn ceremonies, wherever they were celebrated. For the individual person, the ceremonies and ritual received their crowning triumph when, having poured his very heart into what he had experienced in image in the ceremonies, he himself went forth on the pilgrimage to the grave of the redeemer. Certain schools here and there in Asia were still able to grasp the concepts that had been revealed by the ancient Egyptians from contemplation of the mummy, of the mummified human corpse, but this knowledge had passed from the awareness of the general population. Human understanding was incapable of grasping what is at once the mystery of the human being and of the divine world.

And so in the days of Pope Nicholas I, the farther one looked to the East, the more clearly did one see this inward, heartfelt veneration of the cult; people clung passionately to the cult and to all the experiences evoked by the sacred acts, regarding as the crowning triumph of these experiences, indeed as the supreme act of worship, the pilgrimage to the Holy Sepulchre.

Looking over to the East from ninth-century Rome in the days of Nicholas I, there arose the picture of the one influence of which Nicholas I and his counsellors said: this is not for the peoples of Europe, of central and western Europe, for they possess too much of the intellect that is now storming into human evolution to be able to cling, with whatever fervour of the heart, to the mere contemplation of the ceremonial acts and to the actual pilgrimage to the Holy Sepulchre. In the people of Europe there is too much of the dawning intellect to enable them in this way to be fully human beings. It was perceived that although this was possible in the East, it was not to be expected of the peoples of central Europe and the West.

Meanwhile the first great question still remained. Terrible danger seemed imminent if Europe were swept by the stream charged with such deep esotericism, with so much that can be fully grasped only by a spiritualized thinking.

Let me put it like this. Looking from the Rome of Pope Nicholas I towards the West, danger loomed; looking towards the East, more danger. The stream spread out in the East and making its way far into Europe was seen, in reality, as a series of streams, as the stream of the esoteric cult in contrast to the other (western) stream of esoteric life. Central Europe must not, dare not be seized by either stream: this, or something like it, was what was being said at the papal court of Nicholas I. What, then, must be done? The great treasure perceptible to those truly belonging to this first esoteric stream must be clothed in dogma. Words must be found, formulae coined and proclaimed; but the possibility of understanding through actual vision what was thus proclaimed must be withheld from human beings.

The idea of faith was born—the concept that, without providing them with the means of vision, human beings must be given those things in which they can believe in the forms of abstract dogma.

And so a third stream arose, taking hold of the religious
and also the scientific life of central and western Europe. The
onset of the intellect was opposed by dogmas, dogmas that
could not be described as visions reformulated as ideas, but
from which the element of vision had been removed altogether; they were simply believed.

If that esoteric stream which penetrated to Ireland and
died away in later times had been pursued in deed and truth,
the souls of those belonging to it would inevitably have
experienced union with the spiritual world. For the great
question living in this esoteric stream was in reality this: how
can the human being find his orientation in the etheric world,
in the etheric cosmos? The visions which also included the
conception of the mystery of Golgotha as I described it just
now were connected with the etheric cosmos. Here, then, the
great issue was the question concerning the nature of the
etheric cosmos.

But in the middle stream which until far into the Middle
Ages was clothed for the most part in Latinized forms of
thought, the knowledge bearing upon the etheric cosmos
became the content of dogma.

Just as in the West the question concerning the mystery of
the etheric cosmos was an unconscious one, so in the East
there had arisen the great, unconscious question as to the
nature of the etheric organism, the etheric body of the human
being. Unconsciously stirring in all those trends of feeling
and knowledge in the East which poured into cult, ceremony
and ritual was the question: how is the human being to adjust
himself to the workings of his etheric body? Just as in the
South and West the question was: how is the human being to

adjust himself to the etheric cosmos? In earlier times the truth of the supersensory world had been within the human being's reach as an outcome of his natural, dreamlike clairvoyance. It was not necessary for him to become conscious of the etheric in the cosmos and in his own being. A significant feature of the modern age was the great question which now arose concerning the nature and content of the etheric world—in the West, the question as to the etheric cosmos; in the East as to the human being's own etheric body.

The question concerning the etheric cosmos demands the exercise of supreme spiritual effort. Human beings must unfold thought to its highest potency if they are to penetrate the mysteries of the cosmos. In the lecture yesterday I told you that the way is opened up by study of Goethe's conception of plant metamorphosis, but that this must pass on to the mighty metamorphosis which leads over from one earthly life to the next. But in Rome, especially at the time of Pope Nicholas I, this was considered to be full of danger—the living content of this stream must be stifled and concealed.

The Eastern stream too was involved in the struggle concerning the etheric world but particularly the etheric nature of the human being, the etheric body of the human being. With his physical body, the human being lives in contact with the outer world of nature, with the animals, plants and minerals, machines and the like. But to live in and through the etheric body during his existence here on earth is only possible for the human being by the external means presented by ceremony and ritual, by participation in happenings and actions which are not, in the earthly and material sense, real. In the East, human beings longed to share in these acts in order that they might thereby experience the inner nature and working of their own etheric organism.

In the Rome of Pope Nicholas I, this too was considered unsuitable for Europe. It was decided to retain in the West only what the intellect had formulated into a body of dogmas—in which supersensory truths are matters of faith alone, no longer of actual vision. The dogmas were then promulgated over wider areas of the West and the esoteric stream was entirely obscured. The inner attraction to cult and ritual that had characterized eastern Europe was also thought to be out of keeping with the nature of the peoples of central and western Europe, and from this was born the modified form of the cult which now exists in the Roman Catholic Church.

If you compare the cult and ritual of the Eastern Church, the Orthodox Russian Church, with the form of cult practised in the Roman Catholic Church, you will perceive this difference: in the Roman Catholic Church it is more of the nature of a symbol for the eyes to contemplate; in the East it is something into which the soul penetrates with ardent devotion. In the West, people grew increasingly aware of the need to turn away from the cult—wedded as it now was to dogmatic interpretation—to the dogmas, and to explain the cult from the point of view of the dogmas. In the East, cult and ritual worked as a power in themselves and what found its way over to the West was gradually confined within the externalized forms preserved in various occult communities. These communities exist to this very day and though emptied of all the esotericism of olden time, still play no insignificant a part in affairs.

How to inaugurate in Europe a form of cult which does

not, as in the East, take hold of the etheric nature of the human being, and to establish a system of dogma which would make it unnecessary for human beings to direct their gaze to the spiritual world, how to inaugurate a twofold stream of this character—such was the third great question confronting Nicholas I. And at this he laboured.

The outcome of it all was the complete severance of the Eastern, Greek Church, from the Roman Catholic Church. Here, in what I have indicated, lie the inner reasons.

All that I have just been describing to you was still clearly perceptible in the middle of the ninth century, at the time of Pope Nicholas I. In the West, vestiges of esotericism still survived. In Spain particularly, but also in France and in Ireland, esoteric schools existed. There were people who could still look into the spiritual worlds, whose under-standing of Christianity derived from actual vision. Later on, nothing remained of this earlier power of vision save a hint, save those mysterious, repeated glimpses of the Holy Grail or its secular reflection and counterpart, King Arthur's Round Table. There people did feel the presence of something actually connected with vision of worlds beyond the earth, with living experience of these worlds.

Central Europe, extending into those regions of the West where esotericism still survived, was the home of devout belief sustained by dogmas, combined with a world of cere-monies and rites not quite connected with the human etheric body. Of what was living in the East, I have already spoken. Any true portrayal of the life of soul as it was in Europe during the ninth century would have to include a description of these three different soul moods in their many variations.

The account given by history is no more than a cursory, superficial expression of what was actually reigning in the depths. But as time went on, the esoteric stream was followed by a current which, in the forms of Arabian thought, was becoming increasingly exoteric and formal. What human beings in Asia had made of the Aristotelian teachings—that too flowed over in the wake of what had once been a very spiritual understanding, and under this influence the content of this esoteric stream became more and more materialistic. Already in the eleventh and twelfth centuries we see how esotericism begins to flicker and disappear, to melt away as it were; this esoteric stream itself takes on a materialistic mode of thinking, that mode of thinking which in later metamorphosis becomes the materialism of natural science, which has its real origin in Arabian thought.

The middle stream—actually brought into being by Nicholas I but previously fostered by Boniface and supported by the Merovingians and Carolingians—although for long centuries bearing faint traces of the influence exercised by the Grail and other sacred tales in turning the eyes of the soul to the supersensory world, this middle stream tended more and more to introduce the element of materialism into cult and dogma. The older and purer conceptions of transubstantiation, of the celebration of the Mass, for example, were followed by those crude, materialistic conceptions which alone could have resulted in controversy over the Eucharist. When these quarrels arose they were proof of the fact that people no longer understood the Eucharist as originally conceived. Indeed it is a mystery that can be understood only in the light of spiritual knowledge.

And so materialism found its way into the stream that had flowed across to the West from the South and East ; it found its way into the middle stream, and, fundamentally, also into the eastern stream. The waves of materialism were surging forward, and everywhere human beings strove to dam them back as best they could.

We pass now from the ninth century, from the days of Pope Nicholas I, to the eleventh century. We must picture the three great questions facing a man like Pope Nicholas I like three terrible powers, soul-torturing powers. For he could not say— as would be the cases in congresses later on, when frontiers were drawn on maps according to opinions based upon external considerations—he could not say: I decree that there shall be a frontier here, and another frontier here, for souls cannot be divided off in this way. What he could do was to indicate lines of direction and provide the middle stream with a certain strength, and that is where his genius was particularly effective. Nevertheless, the mood prevailing in the East spread far, far into the West. What mood? The mood in which the etheric organism of the human being is set aflame from within by the sacred acts of cult and ritual and in which, in a way more characteristic of western Europe, these acts were now linked with their centre in Jerusalem.

With all the ardour for pilgrimage and the intense yearning for the real centre in Jerusalem, Peter of Amiens, with less effect at the beginning, and then, later on, Bernard of Clairvaux with truly blinding fervour, preached the Cross. With this mood of ardour in Europe there mingled the remains of the stream which had been kept alive in the West by the cult of the Grail, by the Arthurian cult[25]—the remains of the esotericism which had here found its outlet—and there arose the picture of the human being in his physical form as a being to whom the earth is not really earth, but a particular place in the cosmos.

Some such conception was alive in the world of chivalry and knighthood, or at least in that part of it which took shape in western and central Europe, and allied itself with the crusading spirit. And as a faint undertone only, but steadily increasing in strength as the Crusades proceeded, there mingled with this mood the state of mind that had been engendered by Nicholas I as appropriate for European civilization. That is why there is something about the Crusades which is not fully explained by later circumstances. The middle stream spread out and beside it the stream belonging to the east of Europe, regarded in Europe itself as a backward tendency in religion. The western stream converted itself into branches of the occult, esoteric life, into all kinds of occult societies, masonic orders and the like. In the world of scholasticism the middle stream finally laid hold of science too, and then of the child of scholasticism: natural science in its later form.

The spirit inspiring the Crusades cannot be understood by those who look only at what happened in later times; it can be understood only by those who perceive the effects of these impulses from the fourth and fifth centuries of the Christian era on the twelfth and thirteenth centuries, and who grasp the full significance of the question with which Nicholas I, in the ninth century, was so profoundly concerned: how can events in the outer world—in which the human being himself participates, pre-eminent among them being the sacred acts of the cult—how can these be brought into connection with the living flow of spiritual life, with the life of spiritual beings? In the ninth, tenth, and eleventh centuries, the problem had already been set for the peoples of Europe. Just as on the one side they had lost the realities contained in cult and ritual, so too, on the other side, they had lost the realities yielded by spiritual vision. Just as in the East the realities of cult and ritual vanished into the mists of Asia and the conquests of the Turks sealed off the holy place around which the acts of the Christian cult must be centred, so, if I may use a metaphor, did the esoteric secrets contained in the western stream disappear into the Atlantic Ocean. And there arose as a reaction the mood which asked: how are the sacred acts of the cult, with their centre in Jerusalem, to be infused with spiritual life?

Anyone who reads the sermons of Bernard of Clairvaux can feel to this day how, on the one hand, fervent devotion to the cult, to the outer symbol in which the esoteric is contained, speaks from his lips, and how, on the other hand, his heart is fired through and through by all that once stirred in the esotericism of the West. Resounding in the tone and tenor of the sermons of Bernard of Clairvaux, not in what he actually says but in the artistic grandeur and majesty of his utterances, are those mysteries which the etheric cosmos would like to reveal to the human being and can no longer do so, and on the other side all that strives from out of the earth to work in the human being's own etheric body. That is what drove human beings over to Asia, seeking for what they had lost in the West.

Esotericism, however, was really the driving force. By

making a new link with the grave of the redeemer, people wanted to glimpse again what the West had lost. The tragedy of the ensuing age was that this was not understood, that there were no ears ready to listen, let us say, to Rosicrucianism—I mean Rosicrucianism in its genuine form—which sought for Christ in heights of the spirit, not at the physical grave.

Now, however, the time had come for humankind to realize that just as those were told who came to the tomb after the redeemer's death: he whom ye seek is no longer here, seek him elsewhere, so, too, it was said to the crusaders : he whom ye seek is no longer here, seek him elsewhere.

The age is upon us when he who is no longer here must be sought elsewhere, when he must be sought through a new revelation of the spiritual worlds. That is the task of those who are living at this present time and of that I wished to speak to you in connection with our recent studies.

2. The Templars and the Church of Rome (excerpt)

28 December 1904

In this short extract we find unexpectedly stressed the opposition to the Roman Church which the Templars seemed to manifest. It shows that we have moved some way since 1904, when it was barely acceptable to discuss the Order at all. We could ponder on the changes since then which have made this now a topic about which people desire to learn more.

It was at that time, too, that the two great orders of monks were established which played a particularly important role in spiritual life, the Dominicans and the Franciscans. The Dominicans represented the spiritual direction which has been described as Realism[26] whereas the Franciscans tended towards Nominalism. Spiritual orders of knights were established in the Holy Land. The Knights of St John were initially founded to care for the sick.

The second order of knights, the Templars, grew from a mood similar to that which I described as the mood of Godfrey of Bouillon.[20] The Order's real aims were kept secret but through activists working in the background it soon grew very powerful. It was dominated by an anti-Rome outlook which was also in evidence among the Dominicans who frequently found themselves in complete opposition to

Rome. As regards the dogma of the immaculate conception, for example, they fiercely resisted the Pope. The Templars were striving for a purification of Christianity. Taking their cue from John the Baptist, they represented an ascetic tendency. Their acts of worship were so anticlerical as a result of their resistance against the secularization of Rome that it is still not possible to talk publicly about the subject even today. Because of its power, the Order became very awkward for the clergy and the princes so that it suffered severe persecution and was eventually destroyed after the last Grand Master, Jacques de Molay, suffered a martyr's death in 1314 with a number of his fellow Knights.

3. The Templars as initiates of the Grail (excerpt)

1904

This extract has been included for the remarkable statement that the Templars were 'initiated by the Grail'. See the introduction for an attempt to understand this. Steiner speaks further of Lohengrin in an unpublished lecture of 3 December 1905.[27] The Grail stories were really looking ahead to the period from 1413, the age of the consciousness soul or fifth post-Atlantean epoch (in this extract, Steiner uses the older Theosophical terminology of fifth sub-race), in which the individual human ego would really come into its own. He saw the Germanic peoples as predominately the bearers for this, with the English-speaking peoples as having the task of developing the necessary soul forces of independence and objectivity to carry it. John the Baptist and the future age of Aquarius is a pointer to the next period, the sixth post-Atlantean epoch, in which a higher stage of development, the spirit-self, will predominate, resulting in an age of true brother and sisterhood. Thus the spiritual aims of the Templars reached far into the future, and the Grail stories, which were written down during their period, contained imaginative pictures of the qualities needed for the future.

The opposition to the Church is mentioned also, and the fact that the Templars cultivated a star wisdom. This is not clear from historical records and must therefore have been pursued in secrecy. Some of the geometrical alignments connected to the surviving churches may be a hint of this.

A new impulse and a new opportunity were created through the initiate who is given the name of 'Lohengrin'.[27] The conditions under which this initiation look place were very complicated, something which applied to all initiations from that point on, because this impulse had to be brought together with the original stream of Christianity which had developed continuously from Dionysus the Areopagite[28] onwards through Scotus Erigena to scholasticism and mysticism. Although this stream was still able to affect people through the sermons which were preached, it was losing its effect among ordinary people because it required the very highest levels of thought. That is why it had to be fertilized from the original spiritual element. A peak had been reached but it was at the same time a blind alley, and in order to work upon the initiate 'Lohengrin' it had to be fertilized from the East, something that was brought about by the Crusades. The key thing to emerge from this were the Knights Templar, the actual messengers of the Grail. They built a centre of wisdom on the site of Solomon's Temple and after preparation there they became servants of the Holy Grail, were initiated there by the Grail. This happened at the turn from 1200's → the thirteenth to the fourteenth century and was prepared in 1300's the eleventh and twelfth centuries.

We have now reached the stage of preparation for the fifth sub-race, the Germanic-English. The Templar rites show us that it was a matter of bringing the influence of Christianity to bear upon a new race. This enables us to understand the creed of the Knights Templar and their secret cult. They said: 'Christ as represented by the western Church means nothing to us. But we proclaim the Christ who walked in Jerusalem and received initiation through the Baptist; therefore our teachers about Christ are not the teachers and fathers of the Church but John, the initiator himself is our teacher'. That was one principle. Another was: 'We believe once more in the elemental forces that are present in the world. We believe that the destinies of human beings are the result of the stellar constellations and that human beings themselves are born out of these constellations in conformity with the laws of nature'. The civilization of the Germanic-English race has grown out of these two principles: on the one hand the religious Protestant element, on the other the scientific approach to the physical world.

4. The Templars and the forces of evil

25 September 1916 & 2 October 1916

In these two lectures Steiner makes the spiritual background to the Templars very clear, how they identified with the blood of Christ, and that their spiritual endeavours had an effect in combating materialism. The first of the two is set against the horrific practices of some of the old Mexican mysteries, preceding the Aztec civilization but carrying on into it, as the Spanish discovered. The implication is that King Philip the Fair was in some sense connected to these and was thus inspired by evil forces to plot the Templars' downfall. It is here that Steiner mentions the inspiration for the Parsifal epic and also a later influence upon Goethe.

He also refers to the beginnings of a 'threefold' system for social life, and how this came to pass in a distorted way during the French Revolution.

Both lectures contain a surprising reference to the discovery of electricity and the earth's magnetism and, in the second one, the mystery of the etheric or life forces. Is Steiner hinting at something here? It has been suggested that the Templars had knowledge of geomancy, the science of where to locate a site, so could they also have had an understanding for the more subtle energies themselves? Were the 'pilgrim paths' they sought to protect really 'earth energy' currents? Or both? Is he also pointing to the knowledge of the 'double' and its connection to earth forces, as shown in his lectures Secret Brotherhoods?[30] *There is also the belief (not mentioned here but referred to in the Introduction) that some Templars visited the Americas. If we ponder these things, we can begin to make more connections.*

The verses by Anastasius Grün[43] which he read out, also point to the Johannine Rosicrucian aspect of the Templars (who bridged this and the Manichaean stream), the Rose Cross, and the ideal of the New Jerusalem. In May 1912[43a] he had read out verses from Grün's poem 'The Five Easters', which was based on the possibly Rosicrucian legend that every Easter the Master Jesus (in whom the Christ was incorporated) seeks out the places where the events of the first Easter took place, and meets with his pupils, whether or not he is currently incarnated. One of the five meetings described by Grün takes place after the capture of Jerusalem by the Crusaders. The point is that Steiner was not digressing, but introducing material with subtle esoteric connections to his main theme.

In the second lecture his discussion of the role of evil, and the way in which adversary powers can make use of human weaknesses in order to enhance materialism, is most significant for gaining a better understanding. Both good and bad deeds are released into the world at death due to the gradual dissolving of the etheric body. The description of how a soul descends to earth and draws in the necessary etheric (life) forces mentions how a full knowledge of this cannot yet be revealed to humanity.

25 September 1916:

We have been occupied in showing how those spiritual forces that we call the luciferic and ahrimanic powers play their part in the historical growth of humankind. We have seen how what is to be carried over from one age into another in the course of world evolution is carried over through such powers, and we have been at pains to show how in the desires, instincts and strivings for knowledge, in the impulses, too, of the human being's social life, something is present that can only be grasped concretely when one recognizes those supersensory forces that underlie world historical evolution. We have seen how what must come to expression in our fifth post-Atlantean epoch has been in preparation since the fifteenth century. We have seen what new faculties of humankind have evolved in the whole European cultural life since that time.

If we wish to find a spirit who has brought to expression in the most concentrated and clearest manner what the impulses of our time ought to be, then we can look to Goethe. We have already observed that equally in his conception of nature and in his imaginative world, Goethe has expressed something that can form the beginning of the fifth post-Atlantean epoch. I must remind you today how I have often pointed out that Goethe has expressed in intimate fashion in his *Fairy Tale of the Green Snake and the Beautiful Lily*[31] what he regarded as the right impulses of culture, knowledge, feeling and will; that is, what he was obliged to look upon as necessary for the activity of human beings in the future. He has concealed in his fairy tale what he knew of the spiritually hidden active forces at work in humankind since the fifteenth century, and that will be at work for about two thousand years more.

You know, too, how in our Mystery Dramas[32] [see note 7 in Sources] we have sought to bring to life in all possible detail what Goethe saw when he composed his *Fairy Tale of the Green Snake and the Beautiful Lily*. The intention was to bring to expression, in the way in which it can again be brought to expression today, a hundred years later, what inspired Goethe and is to inspire the entire fifth post-

Atlantean culture as the highest spiritual treasure. Such depths of soul underlying so great and powerful a work as *The Fairy Tale of the Green Snake and the Beautiful Lily*, in spite of its being symbolic, and such great impulses underlying Goethe's Faust as a poem of humankind, point again and again to forces lying deep below the surface of consciousness. All this worked in such a soul out of the depths of old cultural impulses. Today I should like to speak a little about such cultural impulses in connection with yesterday's lecture, and of how they went through a kind of spiritualizing process in Goethe.

We must go back to that age in which the impulses for the fifth post-Atlantean epoch were first laid down in germ, back before the fifteenth century because things that are to develop spiritually must be prepared long beforehand. One can only recognize how in the European life of soul, as well as in the European social life, in the striving toward the True, the Beautiful and the Good, the normally progressive divine-spiritual forces intermingle in our age with luciferic-ahrimanic powers when one goes back into the time when the earliest impulses were given. We learned about these first impulses of earlier ages yesterday. Today, we will learn about a similar impetus from the middle of medieval times, and come to know how certain spiritual tendencies were born out of human evolution. In doing so, we will no more than indicate the historical background since nowadays one can read about it in any encyclopaedia.

In order to describe the configuration of the cultural impulses that underwent a certain spiritualization in Goethe, I must refer to the age in which the impulse of the Crusades arose out of European intent; in fact, out of the Christian impulses of European intent. At the time when the intent to visit the Holy Places originated in the civilized inhabitants of Europe there were bitter conflicts in the life there between what are called the luciferic and ahrimanic powers. That is to say, those powers influenced, from the direction that was described yesterday, the progressive, good, truly Christian impulses. They worked in the way in which they are permitted by the wise guidance of the world. Thus, what happens in the wise guidance of the world may be duly influenced by other impulses working from the past and interpenetrating the impulses of the present in the way we have described.

Among much that brings rejoicing to the soul, among much that originated soon after the crusaders won their first successes, we see the founding of the Order of the Knights Templar in the year 1119. Five French knights[33] united under the leadership of Hugo de Payens and, at the holy place where the Mystery of Golgotha occurred, they founded an order dedicated entirely to the Mystery of Golgotha. Its first important home was close to the place where Solomon's Temple once stood, so that the holy wisdom from most ancient times and the wisdom of Solomon could work together for Christianity in this spot with all the feelings and sentiments that arose from the complete and holy devotion to the Mystery of Golgotha and its bearer. In addition to the religious vows of duty to their spiritual superiors usual at that time, the first Knights Templar pledged themselves to work together in the most intensive manner to bring under European control the place where the events of the Mystery of Golgotha had occurred.

The written and unwritten rules of the Order were such that the Knights were to think of nothing except how they could completely fill themselves in heart and soul with the sacred Mystery of Golgotha, and how with every drop of their blood they could help bring the holy places within the sphere of influence of European authority. In each moment of their lives they were to think and feel dedicated with all their strength to this task alone, shunning nothing in order to realize it. Their blood was no longer to be their own but was to be devoted solely to the task we have indicated. Were they to meet a power three times as great as themselves, it was commanded that they were not to flee but were to stand firm. In each moment of their lives they were to think that the blood coursing in their veins did not belong to them but to their great spiritual mission. Whatever wealth they might acquire belonged to no one individual but to the Order alone. Should a member of the Order be killed, no booty should be available to the enemy except the hempen cord girding his loins. This cord was the sign of their work, which was freely undertaken for what was then regarded as the healing of the European spirit. A great and mighty task was set, not so much addressing thought than deep feeling, which aimed at strengthening the individual and personal soul life with the intention that it might be entirely absorbed in the progressive stream of Christian evolution.

This was the star, as it were, that was to shine before the Knights Templar in all that they thought, felt and understood. With this an impulse was given, which in its broader activity—on the wider extension of the Templar Order from Jerusalem over the countries of Europe—should have led to a certain penetration of European life by a Christian spirit. With respect to the immeasurable zeal that existed in the souls of these knights, the powers who have to hold evolution back, leading souls to become estranged from the earth and guided away from it to a special planet, leaving the earth uninhabited, those powers who desired this, set to work quite especially on souls who felt and thought as did the Knights Templar. They desired to devote themselves entirely to the spirit and could easily be attacked by those forces that wished to carry away the spiritual from the earth. These forces do not want the spiritual to be spread over the earth to permeate earth existence. Indeed, the danger is always at hand that souls will become estranged from the earth, become earth weary, and that earthly humanity will become mechanized.

We have a powerfully aspiring spiritual life that we can assume will easily be subject to attempted luciferic temptation; a foothold is here given the latter. Then, however, we also have at the same time as the spread of the Templar Order over the various countries of Europe the possibility of a sharp intrusion of ahrimanic powers in western Europe. At the close of the thirteenth and the beginning of the fourteenth century, when the Templar Order—not the individual Knights but the Order—had attained great prestige and wealth through its activity and had spread over western Europe, we have a human personality ruling the West who can actually be said to have experienced in his soul a kind of inspiration through the moral, or the immoral, power of gold. He was a man who could definitely use for his inspiration the wisdom materialized from gold. Recollect *The Fairy Tale of the Green Snake and the Beautiful Lily* in which the Golden

King became the representative of wisdom. Since spiritual forces also exist in the various substances, which are always only maya with spiritual forces standing behind that the materialist cannot perceive, it is absolutely possible for gold to become an inspirer.

A highly gifted personality, Philip the Fair, who was equipped with an extraordinary degree of cunning and the most evil ahrimanic wisdom, had access to such inspiration through gold. Philip IV, who reigned in France from 1285 to 1314, can really be said to have had a genius for avarice. He felt the instinctive urge to recognize nothing else in the world but what can be paid for with gold, and he was willing to concede power over gold to no one but himself. He wished to bring forcibly under his control all the power that can be exercised through gold. This grew in him to be the immense passion that has become famous in history. When Pope Boniface[34] forbade the French clergy to pay taxes to the State, this fact, in itself not very important, led Philip to make a law forbidding anyone to take gold and silver out of France. All of it was to remain there, such was his will, and only he was to have control of it. One might say that this was his idiosyncrasy. He sought to keep gold and silver for himself and gave a debased currency to his subjects and others. Uproar and resentment among the people could not prevent him from carrying out this policy, so that, when he made a last attempt to mix as little gold and silver as possible in the coinage, he had to flee, on the occasion of a popular riot, to the temple of the Knights Templar. Driven to do so by his own severe regulations, he had had his treasures deposited for safety with them. He was astounded to see how quickly the Knights calmed the popular uprising. At the same time, he was filled with fear because he had seen how great was the moral power of the Knights over the people, and how little he, who was only inspired by gold, availed against them. The Knights, too, had by this time acquired rich treasure and were immensely wealthy, but according to their rules, they were obliged to place all the riches of the Order in the service of spiritual activity and creative work.

When a passion is as strong as avarice was in Philip the Fair, it compels strong forces to emerge from the soul that have a great influence on the unfolding of the will toward other people. To the nation, Philip counted for little, but he meant much to those who were his vassals, and these constituted a great mass. He also understood how to use his power. Since Pope Boniface had once opposed his will to make the clergy in France pay as much as possible, Philip hatched a plot against him. Boniface was freed by his followers but he died of grief soon after. This was at the time when Philip undertook to bring the entire Church completely under his control, thereby making Church officials mere bondsmen of the royal power in which gold ruled. He thereupon caused the removal of the Pope to Avignon, which marked the beginning of what is often known in history as the 'Babylonian captivity' of the papacy. This lasted from the year 1309 to 1377.

Pope Clement V,[35] former Bishop of Bordeaux, resided in Avignon and was a tool completely in the hands of Philip. Gradually, under the working of Philip's powerful will, he had reached the point of no longer having a will of his own, but used his ecclesiastical power only to serve Philip, carrying out all he wanted. Philip was filled with a passionate desire to make himself master of all the then available wealth. After he had seen what a different significance gold could have in other hands, it was no wonder that he wished above all things to exterminate those other hands, the Knights Templar, so that he might confiscate their gold and possess their treasure himself. Now, I said that such a passion, aroused in such a materialistic way and working so intensely, creates powerful forces in the soul. At the same time, it creates knowledge, although of an ahrimanic kind. So it was possible for a certain second-hand sort of knowledge to arise in the soul of Philip of those methods that we have seen flame up in the harshest, most horrible way in the Mexican mysteries.[36] The knowledge arose in Philip of what can be brought about by taking life in the correct way, although in a different, more indirect way from that of the Mexican initiates. As if out of deep subconscious impulses, he found the means of incorporating such impulses into humanity's evolution by putting men to death. For this, he needed victims. In a quite remarkable way this devilish instinct of Philip's harmonized with what developed of necessity in the breast of the Knights, resulting from the dedication of their lives to the things I have indicated.

Naturally, where something great and noble arises, as it did among the Knights Templar, much that does not belong—perhaps even immorality—becomes attached to that greatness and nobleness. There were, of course, Knights who could be reproached for all sorts of things; that shall not be denied. But there was nothing of this kind in the spirit on the basis of which the Order was founded, for what the

Knights had accomplished for Jerusalem stood first, and then what could be accomplished for the Christianizing of the whole of European culture. Gradually the Knights spread out in highly influential societies across England, France, Spain, part of Italy and central Europe. They spread everywhere. In each single Knight was developed to the highest degree this complete penetration of the soul with the feeling and experience of the Mystery of Golgotha and of all that is connected with the Christian impulse. The force of this union with the Christ was strong and intense. He was a true Knight Templar who no longer knew anything of himself but when he felt, he let the Christ feel in him; when he thought, he let the Christ think in him; when he was filled with enthusiasm, he let the Christ in him be enthusiastic. They were perhaps few in whom this ideal had worked a complete transformation, a metamorphosis of the soul life, and who had really often brought the soul out of the body and enabled it to live in the spiritual world, but in respect of the entire Order they were, for all that, a considerable number. Something quite remarkable and powerful had thus entered into the circle of the Templar Order without their having known the rules of Christian initiation other than through sacrificial service. At first in the Crusades, then in the spiritual work in Europe, their souls were so inspired by intense devotion to the Christian impulse and the Mystery of Golgotha that consequently many Knights experienced a Christian initiation. We have before us the following event in world history: on the world historical basis of the experience of a number of men, the Christian initiation, which is to say the perception of those spiritual worlds that are accessible to human beings through Christian initiation, arises from the fundamental depths of human development.

Such events always call forth opposing forces, which, indeed, in those times were abundantly at hand. What thus enters the world is not only loved; it is also excessively hated. In Philip, however, there was less hatred than the desire to rid the world of such a society and to steal from it the treasure that had flowed abundantly to it and that was used only in the service of the spirit.

Now in such an initiation as was experienced by a number of the Knights, there is always the possibility of perceiving not only the beneficent, the divine, but also the luciferic and ahrimanic forces. All that draws human beings down into the ahrimanic world and up into the luciferic appears, to the person who goes through such an initiation, side by side with the insight into the normal worlds. The one thus initiated is confronted with all the sufferings, temptations and trials that affect human beings through the powers hostile to good. He has moments in which the good spiritual world disappears before his spiritual gaze, the gaze of his soul, and he sees himself as though imprisoned by what tries to gain power over him. He sees himself in the hands of the ahrimanic-luciferic forces that wish to seize him to gain control of his will, feeling, thinking and sense perception. These, indeed, are spiritual trials that are well-known from the descriptions of those who have seen into the spiritual world.

There were many in the circle of the Knights Templar who could gain a deep insight into the Mystery of Golgotha and its meaning and into Christian symbolism as it had taken shape through the development of the Last Supper.

They beheld as well the deep background of this symbolism. Many a one who in consequence of his Christian initiation could look into the Christian impulses passing through the historical evolution of the European peoples also saw something else; he experienced it in his own soul, as it were, since it always again came over him as a temptation. Recognizing the unconscious capabilities of the human soul, he repeatedly overcame the temptation that showed itself to him. The initiate thus became conscious of it and sought to overcome what otherwise remained in the subconscious. Many Knights learned to know the devilish urge that takes possession of the will and feeling to debase the Mystery of Golgotha. In the dream pictures by which many such initiates were haunted, there appeared in vision the reverse of the veneration of the symbol of the crucifix. This was possible owing to the way in which the initiation had come about, and particularly because the luciferic forces had stood close by with their temptation. He saw in vision how the human soul could become capable of dishonouring the symbol of the cross and the holy ritual of the consecration of the host. He saw those human forces that urge human beings to return to ancient paganism, to worship what the pagans worshipped and to scorn the advance to Christianity. These men knew how the human soul can succumb to such temptation since they had to overcome it consciously.

You are looking here into a life of soul of which outer history relates but little. Philip the Fair, through his ahrimanic gold initiation, also had a correct knowledge of these facts of soul life, even if only instinctively. He knew enough of it, however, to be able to communicate it to his vassals. Now, after a cruel judicial process had been contrived involving all kinds of investigation, a course of action, decided upon beforehand, was begun. Plots were made, instigated by Philip together with his vassals who had been summoned to investigate the Knights. Although the latter were innocent, they were accused of every imaginable vice. One day in France they were suddenly attacked and thrown into prison. During their confinement their treasures were seized.

Trials were now arranged in which, entirely under the influence of Philip, torture was extensively employed. Every Knight to be found was subjected to the severest torture. Here, therefore, torture was also used to take life, the significance of which you have already learned to know. The intention of Philip was to put to the rack as many persons as possible, and the torture was applied in the most cruel way so that many of the harassed Knights lost consciousness. Philip knew that the pictures of the temptations emerged when, in terrible agony on the rack, their consciousness became clouded. He knew: the images of temptation come out! Under his instigation a catechism of leading questions was so arranged that the answers were always suggested in the way the questions were put. The Knights' answers were, of course, given out of a consciousness dulled by the torture. They were asked, 'Have you denied the Host and refrained from speaking the words of Consecration'? In their clouded consciousness the Knights acknowledged these things. The powers opposing the good spoke out of their vision and, whereas in their conscious life they brought the deepest reverence to the symbol of the cross and the crucifix, they now accused themselves of spitting upon it; they accused themselves of the most dreadful crimes, which normally lived in their subconscious as temptations. So from the admissions made by the tortured Knights, the story was fabricated that they had worshipped an idol instead of Christ, an idol of a human head with luminous eyes; that on their admittance to the Order they were subjected to repulsive sexual procedures of the vilest nature; that they did not conduct the transubstantiation in the right way; that they committed the worst sexual offences; that even on their admittance to the Order they foreswore the Mystery of Golgotha. The catechizing had been so well organized that even the Grand Master of the Order had been tortured into making these subconscious avowals.

It is one of the saddest chapters of human history, but one that can only be understood if one sees clearly that behind the veil of what is related by history stand active forces, and that human life is truly a battlefield. Because of lack of time, I will omit all that might be said further on this subject, but it would be easy to show how there is every ostensible reason for condemning the Knights Templar. Many stood by their avowals, many fled; the majority were condemned and, as stated, even the Grand Master, Jacques de Molay, was forced under torture to speak in the way described. Thus it came about that Philip the Fair, Philip IV of France was able to succeed in convincing his vassal, Pope Clement V—it was not difficult—that the Knights had committed the most shameful crimes, that they were the most unchristian heretics. All this the Pope sanctioned with his benediction, and the Order of the Templars was dissolved. Fifty-four Knights, including Jacques de Molay, were burned at the stake. Shortly afterward in other European countries—in England, Spain, then right into Central Europe and Italy—action was also taken against them.

Thus we see how the interpretation of the Mystery of Golgotha and its influence penetrated into the midst of European evolution through the Order of the Templars. In a deeper sense, however, these things must be looked upon as determined by a certain necessity. Humanity was not yet ripe to receive the impulse of wisdom, beauty and strength in the way the Knights desired. Besides, it was determined on grounds we have yet to learn, grounds that lie in the whole spiritual development of Europe, that the spiritual world was not to be attained in the way in which the Templars entered it. It would have been gained too quickly, which is the luciferic way. We actually see here a most important twofold attack of the forces of Lucifer and Ahriman: Lucifer urging the Knights on, driving them into their misfortune, and Ahriman working actively through the inspiration of Philip the Fair. We see here a significant twofold attack effected in world history.

But what lived and worked in the Knights Templar could not be eradicated. Spiritual life cannot be rooted out; it lives and continues to work. With the Knights, notably with the fifty-four who had been burned at the stake through the agency of Philip, many a soul was certainly drawn up into the spiritual world who would still have done much work on the earth in the spirit of the Templar Order, and who would also have attracted pupils to work in the same spirit. But it had to turn out differently. In the spiritual world these souls lived through those experiences they had undergone in the most terrible agonies that were brought about under the influence of the visionary avowals extorted through torture. Their impulses, which now, between their death and their next birth, went out to souls who had since descended, and also to souls who were still above awaiting incarnation, had to metamorphose from the character of an activity in the physical earthly world into spiritual activity. What now came from the souls of the Knights, who had been murdered in this shameful way and who before their death by burning had to undergo the most frightful experience a person can suffer, was to become for many others a principle of inspiration. Powerful impulses were to flow down into humanity. We can prove this in the case of many human souls.

Today, however, we will keep more to the sphere of knowledge and intellect as we have done also in the other examples given in recent days. Inspiration from the cosmic knowledge of the Knights Templar—this was always given. The fact that ultimately people came to look on the Templars as heretics after they had been burned to death is no surprise; nor is it a surprise that people also believed they had committed all sorts of infamous crimes. Had someone wanted to condemn as especially heretical the devils' scene which has just been presented here,[36a] in which Mephistopheles, the Lemures and the fat and thin devils appear, perhaps—I do not know—countless people everywhere would also have considered that as something heretical. The methods of Philip the Fair are, however, no longer employed in the present time. The cosmic wisdom that these Knights possessed has entered many souls. One could cite many examples of how the inspiration of the

Knights Templar has been drawn into souls. I will read you a passage from the poem 'Ahasver' by Julius Mosen[37] which appeared in 1838. As you can read in the lecture cycles, I have often referred to Julius Mosen, the author of the profound poem 'Ritter Wahn' (Knight Chimera). In the very first canto of the third section of 'Ahasver', Mosen leads his hero to those parts of the earth where, in Ceylon [renamed Sri Lanka, 1972] and the neighbouring islands, the region is found that we describe in the cosmology of our spiritual science as the approximate location of Lemurian evolution. This region of the earth is distinguished in a special way. You know that the magnetic north pole is located at a different point from that of the geographic North Pole. Magnetic needles everywhere point toward the magnetic north pole and one can draw magnetic meridians that meet at this point. Up in North America where the magnetic north pole lies, these magnetic meridians go round the earth in straight lines. Remarkably, however, in the Lemurian region the magnetic

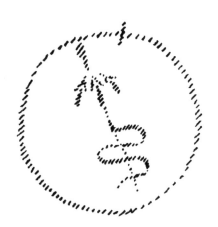

meridians become sinuous serpentine lines. The magnetic
forces are twisted into a serpentine form in this region.
People notice these things far too little today. One who
sees the living earth, however, knows that magnetism is like
a force vivifying the earth; in the north it goes straight, and
in the region of old Lemuria it goes in a tortuous winding
line. Just think how profoundly Julius Mosen speaks as he
sends his Ahasver toward this region in the first canto of
the third epoch—it is divided in epochs—of the poem:

> In line direct and straight from southern pole
> Takes the magnetic line its chosen course,
> When suddenly it twines in serpent-curve
>
> There before India and its neighbour isles
> Before the dungeon where in deepest woe
> Sits the eternal mother ever bound.
>
> In circle form the line drew back its length,
> And twining swift and secret on itself
> With a single plunge in swirling vortex fell.
>
> There the great spirit in a first embrace
> Held the poor spouse, and from their ardent fire
> Sprang the Earth-demons instantly to life.
>
> When thus the first creation came to naught,
> The great, the nameless spirit in his wrath
> Stamped down the bridal couch beneath the sea.

So it goes on. We see inspiration emerge with wonderfully
intuitive knowledge. The wisdom lives on that could only
enter the world amid suffering, torture, persecution and the

most frightful crimes. Nevertheless, it lives on in spiritualized form.

When we seek the most beautiful spiritualization of such wisdom that has become part of the development of Europe, as we have described, then we find one precisely in all that is active and living in the powerful imaginations of Goethe. Goethe knew the secret of the Templars. There is a good reason why he used gold in his *Fairy Tale of the Green Snake and the Beautiful Lily*, in which he made the snake consume the gold and then sacrifice itself. By this deed the gold is wrested from the powers with which Goethe truly knew it must not be allowed to remain. Gold naturally also refers to everything of which gold is a real symbol. Read once more *The Fairy Tale of the Green Snake and the Beautiful Lily* and try to feel how Goethe knew the secret of gold, how, through the way in which he lets gold flow through the fairy tale, he is looking back into earlier times. May I perhaps add here on a personal note that when for the first time in the eighties of the last century I thought about the gold in Goethe's fairy tale, the meaning of the story became clear to me through the way that the gold in it develops.

In the way that Goethe lets gold flow through this fairy tale, he shows how he looks back into the time in which wisdom—for which gold also stands, hence the 'Gold King of Wisdom'—was exposed to such persecution as has been described. Now, he sought to show past, present and future. Goethe saw instinctively into the future of eastern European civilization. He could see how unjustifiable is the way in which the problem of sin and death worked there. If we wished to designate, not quite inappropriately perhaps, the nationality of the man who is led to the Temple and the Beautiful Lily, who appears at first as without vigour as if crippled, then, from what we have said recently about the culture of the East and of Russia, you will not consider it unreasonable to deem this man to be a Russian. In so doing, you will almost certainly follow the line of Goethe's instinct. The secret of European evolution in the fifth post-Atlantean epoch lies concealed within this fairy tale, just as truly as Goethe was able to conceal it in his *Faust*, especially in the second part, as we know from his own statement. It is clearly evident in Goethe—we have already shown it in various respects; later it can be shown in others—that he begins to regard the world and to feel himself in it in accordance with the fundamental demands of the fifth post-Atlantean epoch.

In Goethe we have a true continuation of the life of the Knights Templar but, as I have said, in a spiritualized way. Such a Goethean approach, however, will only be able to enter slowly and gradually into human understanding. I have already shown in certain respects how the impulse for everything of a spiritual scientific nature lies in a Goethean approach. All of spiritual science can be developed from Goethe. I have shown in a public lecture[38] that I gave recently how the first elementary scientific foundation for the doctrine of reincarnation, of repeated earth lives, lies in Goethe's concept of metamorphosis. He begins the teaching of metamorphosis by showing how the leaf changes into the blossom, how an organ appears in different forms. When one follows this through, it contains implicitly what I have often explained here; that is, the head of the human being is the transformed body, and the rest of the body is a human head still to be transformed. Here we have metamorphosis in the ultimate degree, which for science will develop into a direct knowledge of reincarnation, of repeated earth lives. But Goethe is still but little understood; he must first become familiar in the cultural life of humanity. Not only centuries but millennia will be needed in order to unravel what lies in Goethe. As a matter of fact, even today there is no foundation for a study of Goethe, such as a monograph or biography could provide, which has been truly produced in his style.

Let us look at some particular instances in modern culture of attempts to understand Goethe's personality. We can, of course, only cite a few examples. Herman Grimm has, however, rightly said: 'A certain Mr. Lewes[39] has written a book, which was for some time the most famous book on Goethe; some even say the best. It is a book which deals with a personality who was supposed to have been born in Frankfurt am Main in 1749, and to have had a Frankfurt councillor for a father. He then developed and grew up in such a way that Goethe's youth was ascribed to him, along with all sorts of other things taken from Goethe. Goethe's works were attributed to him; he also travelled to Italy in the same year as Goethe, and died the same year Goethe died. This person, however, is not Goethe but a fantasy of Mr. Lewes''.

Then we also have a relatively good book in which Goethe's life and creative work is described with immense industry and better than many other works on Goethe. It is filled, however, from the first to the last page with hatred and aversion. This book is by the Jesuit Alexander Baum-gartner.[40] It is an excellent but, in fact, Jesuitical, book; and antagonistic to Goethe. At least it is better written than the countless others on Goethe that have appeared throughout the nineteenth century and now on into the twentieth. A great number of these works are unpalatable. You continually have to sneeze because the dust of libraries and professors gets up your nose. They have been written by pedants who call what they have produced Goethe. Often they have been written with pedantic pride, but they are also fusty with library dust or the atmosphere you inhale when you guess how often the man who is writing about *Faust*, for example, has opened Grimm's or some other glossary in order to decipher a word or passage—and so on. We might well describe what has been written in this field as horrible, most horrible!

One book, however, stands out in a quite unusual way. This is Herman Grimm's lectures on Goethe given in the seventies at Berlin University. Grimm was, as we can see, a spirit who had the best will and the most wonderful traditions to aid him in familiarizing himself with Goethe. His book is an intelligent and excellent one that has developed right out of the Goethean mood. Grimm grew up in the age when Goethean traditions still existed, but this book shows something quite remarkable. In fact, in a certain respect, it is not a book that has developed from Goethean traditions at all; it is both Goethean and un-Goethean. For Herman Grimm does not write in a Goethean style but, strangely enough, in a style that leads one to think that the book was written by an American, a German American. One can call Grimm's lectures a book written by an American but in German. In style it is American—a style which Grimm has studied. As one of the most enthusiastic followers of Emerson,[41] he has studied him, read, digested, translated him, has completely familiarized himself with him. Now Grimm finds his way into this American-Emerson style so that he is the complete master of it; at the same time he grows enthusiastic about it. One can see at once on reading his novel *Invincible Powers* how he is able to let everything American live on in him. Enthusiasm for what is American and at the same time a wonderful feeling of internationalism emerges in Herman Grimm's Goethe lectures.

In spite of all this, a great deal must happen in the spiritual life of humanity before Goethe and similar spirits will be understood. If sometimes they are properly understood, it happens in quite another way from that of Herman Grimm. Once, in a conversation with him, I tried to make just a few references to the path by which one can gradually enter the spiritual world. The movement of his right arm will remain unforgettable—a gesture of warding off; he wanted to push that aside. He created a Goethe who is simply delightful to see from outside, but one cannot see into his heart. Grimm's Goethe, as he develops as a historical figure, as he stands there, as he moves about and comes into relation with people, as human relations flow into his works, as the contemporary world conception flows into his works—this Goethe goes past our mind's eye like a ghost, a ghost who flits through the world unseen by the living. Goethe will only be understood when we have deepened a Goethean approach to become spiritual science. Then much will emerge from Goethe that he could not express himself. Goethe, truly understood, leads, in fact, to spiritual science, which is really a developed Goethean approach.

From the beginning Goethe also understood that Christianity is a living thing. How he longed for the expressive means to Christianize the modern world conception. It did not lie in his time to find it, but in the new age spiritual science is already working to attain it. Let us take his poem, 'The Mysteries' (*Die Geheimnisse*)[42] in which Brother Mark is guided to the Temple where the Rose Cross is on the door, and let us look at the whole picture. We shall see that the Christian mood is in this fragment, 'The Mysteries', the mood born of the feeling that the symbol of the cross becomes a picture of life through the living roses entwining it! Then, too, Goethe lets his *Faust* end with a Christian conception; he spoke of it to Eckermann in his old age. A time will come when in a much more active, intense sense, one will connect with Christianity the thoughts that ring through the conclusion of *Faust*, although Goethe, who was inwardly modest in such things, was far from doing so himself. He was, in reality, on the way that he made his Brother Mark take—to the cross encircled with roses. In this lies ultimately all that is to flow from such wisdom as was striven for by the Knights Templar. (Their striving was too rapid and unsuitable to physical evolution.)

A longing for the full Christianization of the treasures of wisdom concerning the cosmos and earthly evolution gradually broke through—a longing for the full Christianization of earthly life so that suffering, pain and grief appear as the earth's cross, which then finds its comfort, its elevation, its salvation in the rose symbol of the crucifix. In human beings thus inspired, in whom lived on what was thought to have been destroyed with the burning of the Templars, there repeatedly lived the ideal that in place of what brings strife and quarrels something must appear that can bring good to earth; and this good may be pictured in the symbol of the cross in conjunction with the roses. The book, *Ruins* (*Shutt*), by Anastasius Grün[43] has been given to me today by one of our members. I have here again the same verses that I read to you some time ago to support the fact that this mystery, which this poem also expresses, is not merely something put forward by us, but that it comes to life again and again. Anastasius Grün, the Austrian poet, composed these poems; the eighth edition appeared in 1847. In his own manner he wrote of the progress of humankind, and I will read again today the passage I read years ago[44] as proof of the role played by the image of the rose cross in evolving humanity; that is, among those who are incarnated in the new age. Anastasius Grün turns his gaze toward Palestine and other regions after having described how much confused fighting and quarrelling has been spread over the earth. After he has seen and described much that causes fighting and strife he, who is a great seer in a certain way, turns to a region of the earth that he describes thus. I cannot read all of it as it would take too long, but one's eye is first turned to a part of the earth where the ploughshare is used.

> As children once were digging in a meadow
> They brought a shapeless thing of iron to light,
> It seemed too straight, too heavy for a sickle,
> For plough it was too slender and too slight.

With toil they dragged it home as new found treasure;
The elders see it, yet they know it not;
They call the neighbours round within the circle,
The neighbours see it, yet they know it not.

There is an ancient greybeard, wan and sallow,
Whose lifetime lingers on like tale forgot
Into the present world of busy dealing,
They show it to him, but he knows it not.

Well for them all, that they have never known it,
Else must they weep, and still must be deplored
The folly of their fathers, long since buried,
For what was known by no one was a sword!

Henceforth it shall but cleave the earth as
    ploughshare;
Shall point the seed-corn's path into the ground,
The sword's new hero-deeds are paeaned
When sun-filled airs with song of lark resound.

Once more it came to pass, that in his ploughing
The farmer struck what seemed a piece of stone.
And as his spade unloosed the earthy covers,
A structure of a wondrous shape was shown.

He calls the neighbours round within the circle;
They look at it but still they know it not.
Thou wise and aged one, thou'lt surely tell us?
The greybeard looks at it, yet knows it not.

Thus something was dug up while ploughing and even the
aged man does not recognize it.

Though known to none, yet with its ancient blessing
Eternal in their breast it stands upright,
Scatters its seed around in every roadway;
A Cross it was, this stranger to their sight!

They saw the fight not, and its bloodstained symbol,
They see alone the victory and the crown,
They saw the storm not, and the lashing tempest
They only see the rainbow's glistening shine.

The cross will always be known, even in a region where it was
already buried and pulled out of the earth as a cross of stone,
where civilization has so withdrawn that an unchristian culture has developed. There, Anastasius Grün wishes to say, a
cross is found and human beings know it in their inmost
selves, even though even the oldest among them fails to
recognize it despite all tradition.

Though known to none, yet with its ancient blessing
Eternal in their breast it stands upright,
Scatters its seed around on every roadway;
A Cross it was, this stranger to their sight!

They saw the fight not, and its bloodstained symbol,
They see alone the victory and the crown,
They saw the storm not, and the lashing tempest
They only see the rainbow's glistening shine.

The Cross of stone they set up in the garden;
A venerable relic strange and old,
Flowers of all species lift their growth above it,
While roses climbing high the Cross enfold.

So stands the Cross weighty with solemn meaning
On Golgotha, amidst resplendent sheen;
Long since 'tis hidden by its wealth of roses;
No more, for roses, can the Cross be seen.

But it is there. The cross is there. The roses are there. We only learn the meaning of history when we turn our gaze to what lives in the spiritual and pervades human evolution, when we also turn our attention to the things that show us under what auspices, under what insignia things enter world history. I think that one can feel the deeper connection between what we have characterized as applying to later times and what has been characterized in the ideal of the Knights Templar and their fate in the world at the beginning of the fourteenth century.

2 October 1916:

In the lectures given here for some time, it has been my task to draw attention to certain impulses, certain forces which work in the souls of human beings and from there into all that these souls bring to expression in earthly life. I have spoken about how these impulses and forces developed at the dawn of modern spiritual life. Today, because I want to call your attention to a particular kind of modern spiritual striving, I would like to begin by considering once again an important starting point for modern spiritual life which we have already considered, but which is one of the most important and essential of all. When we enquire into the forces that are at work in modern souls, we are compelled to recognize the importance and significance of this event in history. I refer to the whole destiny and development of the Order of the Knights Templar.

I should like, then, to put before you once more an image of the Order of the Knights Templar in order to show how that which proceeded from this order worked on in broad streams, which still flow into the feelings and perceptions of human beings in our own times.

We know that the Order of the Templars was founded in connection with the Crusades. It was, we might say, an important accompanying phenomenon to that great event in history through which the peoples of Europe sought in their own way to come nearer to the Mystery of Golgotha than they had previously been able to do. The Order of the Templars was founded almost at the very beginning of the Crusades. Leaving on one side all that is known externally about the founding of the Order and the further course of its activity—you can easily read it up in the history books—we find that this Order of the Knights Templar, inwardly considered, expressed an especially deep approach to the Mystery of Golgotha on the part of modern humanity. To begin with, a small number of souls who were faithful and devoted followers of Christianity gathered together at a place that lay near to the ancient Temple of Solomon in Jerusalem and established there a kind of spiritual order. As we have already said, we will not consider now the more external side of the event, but will look at it from a spiritual point of view and turn our attention to what gradually began to live in the souls of the Templars.

According to the purpose of those who founded the Order, they were to turn their minds entirely away from the outward reality of the senses; they were to live among humanity as souls who, even during earthly life, knew how to stand with real inward activity in that life in which—ever since the Mystery of Golgotha—the innermost forces of the human being live through the fact that Christ has united himself with earthly existence. To live in what this earthly life has become through the Mystery of Golgotha, to stand right within that life—this was what was sought and intended for the souls who gathered together in the Order of the Templars.

In their blood, as the agent of that which distinguishes the earthly human being, in their 'I'—but also in all their feeling and thinking, in their very being and existence—these souls were, in a sense, to forget their connection with sensory physical existence. They had to live solely in what streams from the Mystery of Golgotha and fight for the continuance of the strongest impulses that are connected with the Mystery of Golgotha.

The blood of the Templars belonged to Christ Jesus—each one of them knew this. Their blood belonged to nothing else on earth than to Christ Jesus. Every moment of their life was to be filled with the perpetual consciousness of how in their own soul there dwelt—in the words of St Paul—'not I, but Christ in me'! And in bloody and severe combat, in devoted work such as the Crusades demanded, the Templars put into practice what they had spiritually undertaken to do. Words are unable to describe what lived in the souls of these men, who were never allowed to waver in their duty, who were never allowed to flee, even if a force three times their strength confronted them on the physical plane, but who had calmly to await death, the death that they were ready to endure in order to establish more firmly in earth existence the impulse which came from the Mystery of Golgotha. It was an intense life of the whole human being in union with the Mystery of Golgotha.

Now, when such an intense life is lived in the right rhythms so that it can take its place in the whole stream of cosmic and earthly forces, then something of real significance develops out of such a life. I say advisedly: of real significance. When a consciousness such as this is placed with a certain rhythm— inwardly, mystically—into all that goes on in the outside world, then one can have experience again and again of things that bring one's own inner being into connection with the divine and spiritual. But something else, something that has still greater effect is developed when this inner experience, combined with the course of external history, is placed into the service of the outer historical course of events. And it was intended that what lived consciously in the souls of the Knights Templar should be in harmony with what had to be done in the attempt to regain power over the sacred tomb. A deeply mystical life developed in this way among those who belonged to this spiritual order, an order which for this very reason could accomplish more for the world than other spiritual orders. For when life is lived mystically in this way in the context of the life going on in the surrounding world, then what is experienced mystically streams into the invisible and supersensory forces of the world surrounding that human being. It becomes objective; it does not exist merely within the soul of the person concerned, but works on further in the course of history. A mysticism such as this means that an experience of the soul is not simply there for the single human being, but turns into objective forces which were formerly not there in the spiritual stream that carries and upholds humanity; these forces come to birth and are there. When a person performs his daily tasks with his hands or with other implements, he places some external material thing into the world. With a mysticism such as was unfolded by the Knights Templar, something spiritual is added to the spiritual 'effects' of the world. And inasmuch as this took place, humanity was actually brought a stage further in its evolution. This experience of the Templars meant that the Mystery of Golgotha was understood, and also experienced, at a higher stage than before. Something was now present in the world with regard to the Mystery of Golgotha which was previously not there. But the souls of the Templars had at the same time achieved something else.

Through the intense inward penetration of the Mystery of Golgotha they had gained the power actually to achieve Christian initiation by means of the historical event. Christian initiation may be achieved in the manner described in our books, but in this case it was achieved in the following way. Their external deeds and the enthusiasm that lived in these deeds drew out the souls of the Templars so that these souls, being separated from the body, outside the body, lived with the spiritual progress of humanity and penetrated in soul and spirit the secrets of the Mystery of Golgotha. They then underwent many and deep experiences, and not for the individual soul alone but for all humanity.

Then, as we know, the Order of the Knights Templar increased and spread, and in addition to the immensely powerful influence that it possessed spiritually—more in a supersensory manner than by external influences—it acquired great wealth. And I have already described how the time came for these external treasures, which the Knights Templar amassed to a greater and greater extent, to be converted into temporal power. I have told you how through a kind of initiation with the evil principle of gold Philip the Fair was chosen to be the instrument to oppose the Templars. That is to say, he wanted in the first place to possess their treasures. But Philip the Fair knew more than most people in the world. Through what he had experienced he knew many of the secrets of the human soul. And so it came about that Philip the Fair could be a fitting instrument in the service of mephistophelian-ahrimanic powers[45] whose aim and objective it was to render ineffective the Templar movement in the form it had first of all taken.

Philip the Fair was, as we have said, the instrument of other, spiritual, mephistophelian-ahrimanic powers. Under the inspiration of these powers, Philip the Fair knew what it would have meant if what the Templars had acquired as knowledge of the Mystery of Golgotha, and as feelings and impulses of will connected with that mystery, had been allowed to flow into the spiritual streams which flow through the world just as truly as do the outwardly visible events. What had thus developed had therefore to be torn away from the normally progressive divine spiritual powers; it had to be turned to other paths. To this end something else also had to be made to happen, namely that something which could only live in the souls of the Templars should be torn out of their individual selves. Just as that which the Templars had experienced in connection with the Mystery of Golgotha did not remain with them as individuals, but was placed out into the general evolution of humanity, so now something else was also to be removed from them as individuals and embodied in the objective spiritual stream. And this could only be accomplished by means of a particularly cruel deed, a terrible act of cruelty.

The Templars were committed to trial. Not only were they accused of external crimes, of which they were most certainly innocent—as can be proved historically if one is only ready to see the truth—but they were accused above all of blaspheming Christianity, of blaspheming the Mystery of Golgotha itself, of worshipping idols, of introducing paganism into the Mystery of Golgotha, of not using the right formula in the act of consecration at the transubstantiation, indeed, even of desecrating the cross. The Templars were also accused of all kinds of other crimes, even unnatural crimes. And hundreds and hundreds of them were subjected to the cruel torture of the rack.

Those who committed them for trial knew what such torture on the rack meant. The ordinary day consciousness of those who underwent this torture was suppressed, so that during the torture they forgot in their surface consciousness their connection with the Mystery of Golgotha. But they had become acquainted—and this is the case with everyone who really sees into the spiritual world—they had become acquainted with all the trials and temptations which beset human beings when they truly approach the good divine spiritual powers. The Templars had become acquainted with all the enemies who work out of the lower spiritual kingdoms and want to drag the human being down and lead him into evil, beings which are able to work against the good in the impulses and desires and passions, and especially in hatred and mocking and irony. In many, many hours that were for them sacred hours of their life, the Templars had won those inner victories that human beings can win when with open eyes they pass through the worlds that lie beyond the threshold of the world of the senses; for these worlds must first be overcome before the human being can enter with strengthened powers into the spiritual worlds where he rightly belongs.

During their torture, the vision of the Templars that could look out over these spiritual worlds to which they belonged became clouded and dim, their surface consciousness was dulled, and their inner gaze was directed entirely and only to what they had experienced as something to be overcome; was directed to the temptations over which they had gained victory after victory. And thus it came about that during the moments while they were actually being tortured on the rack, they forgot their connection with the Mystery of Golgotha, forgot how with their soul they were living in the spiritual and eternal worlds. The trials and temptations which they had resisted and overcome stood before them, as a vision, while they lay stretched on the rack. And they acknowledged the very thing that each one for himself had overcome, they confessed it to be a custom within the order. They confessed themselves to be guilty of precisely that over which they had again and again been victorious. Every one of these Templars was forced into appearing to be the person within themselves over which they had been inwardly victorious, over which they had to gain victory before they could reach the highest and holiest of all with the assistance of higher forces. (I speak of all true Templars: abuses can of course be found everywhere.)

All this the opponents knew. They knew that just as, on the one hand, the Mystery of Golgotha had been made part of the evolution of humanity as an influence for good, so now, in the same way, what lived in this evil consciousness had by this means been placed outside, objectified and embodied in the evolution of humanity because ordinary consciousness had been dulled. It had become a factor in history.

Two streams were thus allowed to flow into modern history: what the Templars experienced in their holiest moments, what they had worked out and developed within the progressing spiritual stream of humanity. But also what had been wrested from them by Ahriman-Mephistopheles, fetched up out of their consciousness in order to make it objective, in order to form it objectively and make it effective in the further progress of the centuries.

At this point a simple-minded person might easily put the question: Why do the divine spiritual powers allow such a thing to happen? Why do they not guide humankind through the course of history without it having to undergo such a painful trial. Such a thought is 'human, all too human'. It arises in the mind of those who believe that the world would be better if it had been made not by gods but by men. Many people may think this, they may think that with their intellect they can criticize the wisdom that is at work throughout the world. But such a way of thinking leads also to the very extreme of intellectual pride.

We human beings are called upon to penetrate into the secrets of existence, not to criticize the wisdom-filled guidance of the world. We must therefore also gain insight into the role and significance of the evil currents which are permitted by the wise guidance of the world. For if only the good were allowed, if good impulses alone worked in history, human beings would never be so guided in their historical evolution that they could develop freedom. Only through the fact that evil exists in the spiritual course of human history can humanity develop to freedom. And if the gods were to turn away the human being's gaze from evil, he would have to remain for ever an automaton, he would never become free. Things are indeed so ordered in the progress of humanity that even that which causes the deepest sorrow is led at last to good. Pain is only a temporary thing. Not that it is on that account any less great and deep. We must not deceive ourselves as to pain and fall prey to some cheap mysticism that will not see the pain; we must be ready to partake in it, ready to immerse ourselves in it, ready to pour it out over our own soul. But at the same time, without criticizing the spiritual purpose and intent of existence, we must also learn to understand how the most varied impulses of a positive and negative nature are introduced into the evolution of humanity in order that human beings may become not only good but also free and possessors of their own impulses.

And so in the evolution and destiny of the Templars we see an impulse that is of importance for all the succeeding centuries of the modern era. If the purpose of the order had continued to be lived out with the intensity and strength with which it was first lived by the great Templars, succeeding humanity would not have been able to bear it. The speed of evolution had, as it were, to be checked; the stream had to be held back. But in this way it was made more inward. And so we see how in the two streams we have indicated in modern history a deeply inward life developed alongside external materialism. For the mephistophelian impulse which Mephistopheles-Ahriman extracted by force through his instrument Philip the Fair lived on, it lived on together with many other things in the materialistic thoughts and feelings of people and in all the materialistic impulses which appeared among humankind from the fifteenth to the nineteenth century. Hence it has come about that what we know as materialism has spread itself so widely over the soul and spirit of human beings and over all their social life and has prepared the ground for the karma of our own time.

Had things not happened in this way, had the stream of materialism not been allowed to spread so far and wide, our connection with the spiritual world could not have become so deep and intimate either. For what the Templars had accomplished by entering in a living spiritual sense into the Mystery of Golgotha was not lost, it lived on. And after their terrible experiences on the rack—fifty-four Templars were put to death—the souls of the Templars who had passed through the portal of death under these circumstances were now able to send down from the spiritual world streams of spiritual life for those who lived in the succeeding centuries.

Fifty-four Templars were burnt at the stake in 1312.[*] Fifty-four souls ascended into the spiritual worlds. And from that time there began in European humanity a spiritual

---

[*] Historical records give this date as 1310. (Editor's note.)

development—on a supersensory and invisible level, without it being outwardly visible in the facts of history—which owed its origin to the fact that individual souls were continually being inspired from the spiritual world with what these fifty-four souls carried through the gate of death into the spiritual world.

I will relate only one example of this; it is one I have already mentioned before, but I will now deal with it in more detail from another perspective.

Before tragedy overtook the Order of the Templars, a whole century before the year 1312, Wolfram von Eschenbach[23] composed his poem *Parsifal*. Working alone, or only in a very small group, Wolfram von Eschenbach produced this ballad about a soul who strives by means of inward purification for the life which the Knights Templar also held before them continually as their ultimate goal. In a wealth of images and in wonderful imaginations Wolfram von Eschenbach unfolds before our view the inner life of Parsifal, who was for him the representative of the Templar ideal.

Now let us enquire: Do we see any important external result of Parsifal in the historical development of subsequent ages? We do not. In the further history of European humanity it was, as we know, Richard Wagner who first again presented Parsifal, and then in quite another way. But the spiritual power, the spiritual impulse that flowed into the soul of Wolfram von Eschenbach—at that time still from the earth—became in subsequent centuries an inspiration from the spiritual world for many others. And anyone who is able to perceive the mysterious connections between life on earth and spiritual life knows that the impulses which were carried

into the spiritual world through the destiny of the Templars
flowed also into the soul of Goethe. There was a reason why
in the 1780s Goethe began a poem which he never finished.
It is significant that he began it; and it is equally significant
that even he was not strong enough to bring to actual
expression the mighty thought of this poem. I refer to the
poem 'The Mysteries',[42] where the Brother Mark goes to the
lonely castle of the Rosicrucians and enters the circle of the
Twelve. Goethe grasped—in his own way, of course—the
fundamental thought which is also contained in *Parzifal*. But
he was not able to complete it, showing us by that very fact
how all of us are located within the same spiritual development which Goethe experienced only in its beginnings, and
at which we must work and work and work, that we may be
able to give more shape to these beginnings and make greater
and greater progress in the penetration of the spiritual world.
Goethe devoted all his powers to the first beginnings of this
spiritual development, he let them flow into his *Faust* where
he set out to portray the human being's connection with the
forces of the spirit, which include for him the ahrimanic-
mephistophelian forces.

Anyone who observes history in its spiritual development
in concrete terms can see quite clearly that from the spiritual
world there flowed into the soul of Goethe on earth what the
Templars—whose manner of death had been so cruel and so
significant—had taken up into the spiritual worlds and,
precisely because they had gone through the gate of death in
this way, could send down as inspiration into the souls of
human beings. It flowed down not just into Goethe's soul
alone but into many others, even if it achieved greater sig-

nificance in Goethe, and it continues to live although little noticed by people. The spiritual element in *Faust* itself still largely escapes notice in the outside world. It lives on, however, and is progressing towards an ever richer life. It will have to become more and more fruitful if humanity is not to drift into decadence instead of evolving to higher levels. But this lies in our own choice. In our age it is given into the human being's own hands; the choice as to whether he will fall into decadence and continue to cling to materialism or strive upwards into the spiritual worlds is set before him and will be so more and more definitely.

For during the time that we human beings live on earth it is only in our physical body that we live a life connected with the earth. The body that is woven of light and sound and life and is in this physical body, the so-called etheric body, is involved not only in the life of earth but in the life of the cosmos. And when a human soul descends from the spiritual worlds to enter existence through birth, then already before the event forces are directed in the cosmos in a right way to build up the etheric organism of the human being, even as the physical body of the human being is built up from the physical forces and physical substances of earth.

Pride and arrogance lives in the very simplest ideas of human beings, and this is especially true in our materialistic age. In this materialistic age, parents actually believe that they bring their children into existence all by themselves. And as materialism spreads, it will be believed to a greater and greater extent that it is the parents alone who bring the children into existence. Seen spiritually, it is different. Human beings here on earth only provide the opportunity for something spiritual to descend to them. What a person can do as a parent consists solely of preparing the place by means of which an etheric body that is being prepared from out of the far spaces of the cosmos may be able to descend to earth! This etheric organism of the human being is just as much an organized entity as is the physical organism. The physical organism—we see how it has head, arms, hands, trunk and all the parts that anatomists and physiologists describe. For spiritual vision, the etheric organism shines through this physical organism. The physical organism breathes in air and breathes out air. The etheric organism breathes out light and this light it gives to us. And when it breathes out light and confers the light to us we live by means of its light. And it breathes in light. As we breathe air in and out, so does our etheric body breathe light in and out. And when it breathes in light, it uses up the light just as we use up air physically. (You can read about this in my *Mystery Plays* where in a certain section the secret of the etheric world is described in dramatic terms.) The etheric body breathes in light, uses up the light and changes it into darkness. It can then receive into this darkness the sound of the cosmos that lives in the harmony of the spheres; can receive into it the impulses of life. As we receive physical nourishment so the etheric being that lives in us breathes light in and out. As we use up in us the oxygen of the air and generate carbon dioxide, so the etheric body uses up the light, shooting it through with darkness so that colours appear. As a result, the etheric body shows itself to clairvoyant vision in waves of colour. And while the etheric body prepares the light for the darkness and thereby breathes inwardly, it lives in that it receives the sound of the cosmos and changes it into the life of the cosmos. And what we receive in this way as our etheric body comes down to us from the wide and distant spaces of the cosmos at particular times.

Today, it is not yet possible to show in every detail how the human etheric body travels downwards on the paths of light when these paths are guided in a particular manner through the constellation of the stars. For that to be possible, human beings will have to lift themselves up to a higher level of morality, for today this mystery of the descent of human etheric bodies on the paths of light and the harmony of the spheres would be misused by human beings in the most terrible manner. For what is contained in this mystery would, if people of lower impulses wanted to acquire it, give parents unlimited power over all their descendants.[46] Accordingly, you will understand that this mystery of how the etheric bodies come to the human beings who are incarnating, of how they come on the paths of light and the paths of sound from out of the harmony of the spheres will have to remain a mystery for a long time to come. Only under certain quite definite conditions can we learn anything of this mystery, for the failure to comply with the conditions would mean, as I have said, that parents could acquire a hitherto unheard of power over their offspring, who might be completely deprived of all independence, of all personality and of all individuality and have the will of their parents thrust upon them. Wisely this mystery is hidden away for humankind in the unconscious and takes its course there in a good and healthy way, working through the will of the wise guidance of the cosmos.

Our etheric body travels quite a different path from our physical body. After we have passed through the gate of death, we still carry, as you know, our etheric body for a few days. Then we have to return it to the cosmos. In the spiritual sphere, in the cosmos our etheric body remains only as an image for our own further life between death and new birth. But it is incorporated into the cosmos in a variety of ways—in one way when people die early through some accident or otherwise, and in a different way when people live their full life. When we look across into the world that lies beyond the threshold, we know that early death as well as later death both have a great significance in the whole cosmic connection. For our etheric body that we give up continues to work spiritually.

Fundamentally speaking, seen from a deeper aspect, we all grow old. Physically, one person may die earlier than another; seen from a spiritual perspective, we all grow to the same age. If we die early, our physical body comes to an end early but our etheric body lives on in the cosmos. And because we have died early, our etheric body has other functions in the cosmos than if we had died later. When we add together the years that we live in the physical and the etheric body as human beings, we find that everyone lives to about the same age, for we have the deeds on earth that we accomplish in the physical body and we have what we accomplish in the etheric body also after death in the life that we live there not for ourselves but for others, for the world.

But when an event takes place such as happened to the Templars, something different again occurs than in the case of individual lives. The life that we lead as an individual relates to our own person; but there is also the life that can be objectively separated from us. In the case of the Templars this was, on the one hand, what they did for the continuance and spread of the Mystery of Golgotha and, on the other hand, what happened through the actions of mephistophelian-ahrimanic forces in support of the impulse of modern materialism. These things also continue to live on as fragments of the etheric body but they are incorporated into the whole process of history. So that some of the life human beings live in their etheric body lives on further with the human individuality, while some of it is incorporated into the course of history when it has been torn away from the human being in the manner described. And the etheric body is the means or medium by which that which a human being lives in his soul so objectively that it can go out of his soul has something to hold on to, we might say, for its continuing life. That is what the etheric body is.

What flowed into the etheric world from the spiritual impulses of the Templars, lived on etherically. Through this continued etheric life many souls were prepared to receive the inspirations which I have described as coming out of the spiritual world from the souls of the Templars themselves. That is what has actually been taking place in modern times.

However, there began increasingly to enter into what flowed from the souls of the Templars that which comes from mephistophelian-ahrimanic impulses and is steeped in the mephistophelian-ahrimanic element which was inaugurated on the rack where the Templars were tortured to the extent that they were forced to speak untruths about themselves. This fact—not as the only factor but as one of the underlying spiritual reasons for modern materialism—has to be understood if we want to acquire an inner understanding of modern materialistic evolution.

And so it came about in modern times that while certain individuals were inspired with high spiritual truths, culture in general became increasingly materialistic in character. The soul's eye grew dim with regard to what surrounds us on earth in the spiritual sense, and to where we go when we pass through the gate of death and from where we come when we pass through the portal of birth. The human gaze was increasingly turned away from seeing things spiritual; and this was true of all the different spheres of life, the spiritual sphere, the sphere of religion, the sphere of social life. The human being's gaze was increasingly directed to the material world as it revealed itself to his senses and the result has been that since the rise of modern times humankind has fallen into a great many errors.

I must repeat, I am not criticizing this fact, I am not passing judgement on it. The fact that errors found their way into human evolution made human beings experience them. They will gradually learn to understand them, and in over-coming them they will develop stronger forces than they would have had if the path to their goal had been implanted in them automatically. But now the time has come when such insights must be developed and human beings must see how everything material contains impulses of error. Today people are called upon again and again to make up their mind to see through the errors and overcome them.

It is not my intention to apportion blame for anything that has happened in history, what I want to do is to look at history objectively. The events of modern times have brought it about that people's thoughts and feelings run their course only on the basis of external physical reality, only in accordance with what the human being experiences between birth and death. Even religious life has gradually assumed a personal character, inasmuch as it aims merely at putting into a person's hand a means whereby he may find blessing in his own soul. Modern religious life turns people's gaze increasingly away from the reality of the spiritual world, is really permeated with a materialistic outlook. As I have said, I have no intention of casting aspersions on any event in history; the events of history must however be described in such a way that they may be rightly understood—that is, if the coming generation is not to fall into decadence but to take a turn and move upwards.

We see the stream of materialism flow on, and side by side with it the parallel hidden stream. Then, at the end of the eighteenth century, we come to a tremendous event, an event the influence of which was felt throughout the whole of the nineteenth century and right on into the present time. At the end of the eighteenth century we see the French Revolution spread its currents far and wide over European civilization. Many things took their course in the French Revolution as historians have described them. But in addition to what we already know about the French Revolution and the impulse proceeding from it and working on in European history, we must also understand the spiritual effects of materialistic mephistophelian-ahrimanic impulses.

The French Revolution strove for a very high ideal. (As I said before, we are not concerned with finding fault but with understanding the events of history.) And it strove for it in a time which was still subject to the shadow of the event I described today—the event which left Mephistopheles-

Ahriman in a powerful position to inject into European life the impulse of materialism. It may be said of the best of those who were responsible for the French Revolution that they believed in the physical plane alone. It may be that in their consciousness they thought they believed in something else. However, what people profess with words is of little relevance; the important thing is to have a living consciousness in one's soul of what is really working in the world and those who were responsible for the French Revolution were conscious only of the physical plane. They strove, it is true, for a high ideal, but they knew nothing of the trinity in the human being: the body that works in the human being by means of the etheric principle, the soul that works through the astral principle, and the spirit that works in a person to begin with through the ego.

At the end of the eighteenth century the human being was already regarded in the way that he is regarded—to his lasting harm and loss—by modern materialistic physiology and biology. That is to say, even if in a religious sense people had some notion of a spiritual life and perhaps also talked about it, their sight was really only directed at what lives here in the physical world between birth and death. What lives here can be understood. Even that of course is not yet entirely understood; nevertheless one can understand it when one directs one's attention solely to the external physical body. What lives in the entire human being, that can only be understood when it is known that an etheric principle, an astral principle and an ego principle are united with the external physical body.

For even while we are here in the physical world, there lives in us something that is of soul and spirit that belongs to the spiritual worlds. Here we are body, soul and spirit and when we have passed through the gates of death we shall again be threefold human beings, only with another spiritual body. So that anyone who observes and studies the human being living out his life as a physical person between birth and death is not studying the whole human being but is subject to error as far as the whole human being is concerned. If we set up an ideal for the physical human being only, then this ideal cannot be applied to the whole human being. The events that happen in the world must not be looked upon as erroneous in themselves. What makes itself manifest in the world is indeed truth. But the way in which people regard it and turn it into deeds and actions often causes confusion.

And confusion arose in the minds of people at the end of the eighteenth century because everything was applied to the physical body. Ideals which only have meaning when the human being is seen as a trinity were aspired for as the ideals for a purely physical single entity. And so it came about that lofty and beautiful ideals were on everyone's lips in a time when people were not capable of understanding them but only confused and falsified them because they tried to comprehend them as one, believing, as they did, in the physical body alone. In fact, of the threefold ideal of fraternity, liberty and equality, fraternity is the only one that applies to the physical body of the human being. Liberty only has meaning when it refers to the human soul and equality when it refers to the spirit as it lives in the human being, in the 'I'.

Only when we are aware that the human being consists of

body, soul and spirit, and when the three ideals of the end of the eighteenth century are related to their proper counterpart—fraternity to the body, liberty to the soul, and equality to the 'I' or ego—only then do we refer to them in a sense and meaning that is in accord with the inner meaning of the spiritual world. Fraternity we can develop to the extent that we are physical human beings with physical bodies belonging to the earth. When we accept fraternity into our social order, then for the social order on the physical plane fraternity is the right and proper thing.

Liberty can only be acquired by human beings in their soul to the extent that it is with the soul that we incarnate on earth. For liberty is only possible on earth when it relates to the souls of human beings who live in their social order with the purpose of acquiring the faculty to hold the balance between the lower and the higher forces. When we are able, as human beings, to hold the balance between the lower and the higher forces in the human soul, then we develop the forces that can live here between birth and death, and forces too that we need when we pass through the gate of death. So that alongside the social order, a 'soul order' is necessary on earth in which the souls of human beings can take their places individually and are able to develop the forces of liberty which they can take with them through the gates of death, but which they can only take with them if they have prepared themselves for the life after death in this life here. The kind of true interaction between souls should be established on earth which allows souls to develop the forces of freedom, which allows all human events great and small and all attempts to give form to human activity and creation to have as their aim that the human being holds the balance in his soul with regard to what lives and works spiritually. This must come to be an ideal.

The human being becomes free when he is in a position to acquire these soul forces in the external physical world as, for example, he can acquire them when he is able to follow the beautiful forms that live in an art that has its true source in the spirit. The human being becomes free when there is interchange and communion between two souls of such a nature that the one soul is able to follow the other with ever-growing understanding and with ever-growing love. If it is the human physical body with which we are concerned, then fraternity comes into play; if it is a question of the soul, then we have to look for the forging of those delicate and subtle links that arise between soul and soul, that must find their way right into the structure of our life on earth and must always work towards engendering interest, deep interest, in one soul for the other. For in this way alone can souls become free—and it is only souls that can become free.

Equality applied to the external physical world is nonsense, for such equality would mean uniformity. Everything in the world undergoes change; everything in the world exists in many different forms; everything in the world comes to expression in multiplicity and diversity. That is why the physical world exists, in order that the spiritual may go through a multitude of forms. But in all the multiple and manifold life of the human being, one thing remains constant because it is still in its beginning. Whereas we have carried everything in our human nature except the 'I' or ego in us since the Saturn, Sun and Moon periods, we have the 'I' or ego for the first time in this life on earth. The 'I' is only in its beginnings. During the whole of our life between birth and death we come no further in the spiritual sphere than to say to ourselves 'I' and to take cognizance of this 'I'. We can only observe the 'I' either when through initiation we are outside the body here between birth and death or when we have passed through the gate of death and it is given us to look back in memory on our earth body and behold the 'I' spiritually. But in this 'I' all possible variety comes to expression on the earth. And our life on earth must be so constructed as to give possibility for all the variety that can enter earth life in human individuality to come to expression. One human being manifests this kind individuality, another that, and a third a different one again. All these individualities in their several workings are focussed in a point—in the point of the ego or 'I'. There we are alike and through this focal point where we are alike can pass all that we communicate to one another as spirits. The fact that we all have this 'I' point where we are alike provides the possibility for the development in humankind of a community life. That which is different in all of us passes through what is alike. Consequently spiritual equality is not the establishment of what is contributed by the single human individual to the whole stream of cosmic spiritual evolution; rather it is because what has placed each of us into a different kind of life passes through our 'I', through the spiritual in us, that it becomes something that can be shared by all, it flows on as a common good in the stream of cosmic evolution. Equality belongs properly to the spirit.

No generation of human beings will understand how the

three ideals of fraternity, liberty and equality can come to realization in the life of humankind unless they understand that the human being carries in him this trinity of body, soul and spirit. That human beings were unable in the eighteenth century, and have continued to be unable throughout the nineteenth century, to understand this was a result of the strength of the ahrimanic-mephistophelian stream which entered modern evolution in the way I have described. The eighteenth century mixed up equality, liberty and fraternity and applied all three to external physical life. The way this was understood in the nineteenth century can only produce social chaos. And humankind will have to drift further and further into this chaos if it is not given spiritual science and spiritual life, leading to an understanding of the human being as a trinity and a renewal of earthly life for the threefold human being.

The human being, or rather humankind, had to go through materialism. His forces would have been too weak for the times to follow if he had not gone through materialism. Remarkable and amazing is the evolution of humankind!

Let us look back for a moment to an event of the Lemurian[47] epoch. We find there a certain moment in evolution—it lies thousands and thousands of years back—when humankind on earth was quite different from what it is now. You will know from the descriptions I have given of human evolution on the earth in *Occult Science* that the various impulses entered only gradually into the human being. There was a moment in evolution when what we today call magnetic and electric forces established themselves within the human being. For magnetic and electric forces live in us in a mysterious manner. Before this time, human beings lived on earth without the magnetic and electric forces that have developed ever since on a spiritual level between the workings of the nerves and the blood. They were incorporated into the human being at that time. The forces of magnetism we will leave out of consideration, also some forms of the forces of electricity. But the forces which I will distinguish as the electric forces in galvanism, voltaism etc., forces that have taken deep hold in the culture and civilization of our time, these forces entered the human organism in that far-off time and combined with human life; and this very fact made it possible for them to remain for a long time unknown to human consciousness.

The human being carried them within himself and for that very reason they remained unknown to him externally. The forces of magnetism and the other electrical forces were discovered at an earlier stage. Galvanism, electricity resulting from contact, which has a much deeper determining influence on the karma of our age than is generally realized, was, as you know, only discovered at the turn from the eighteenth to the nineteenth century by Galvani and Volta.[48] People give far too little thought to such facts as these. Just consider for a moment. Galvani was dealing with the leg of a frog. 'By chance' as we say, he fastened it to the window and it came in contact with iron and twitched. That was the beginning of all the discoveries that rule the earth today through electric current. And it happened such a short time ago! People do not generally stop to think why it is that humankind did not discover this knowledge sooner. Suddenly this thought emerges in a human being in a perfectly marvellous way; he stumbled on it in a way that is more than accidental. In this materialistic age of ours we naturally never stop to think about such things. And this is the reason why we can understand absolutely nothing at all of the real development of the earth.

The truth of the matter is as follows. After humankind had passed the moment in the Lemurian age when it had implanted into it the forces that pass through the wire today as electricity and work in an invisible manner in the human being himself, after this time had passed, electricity existed inside the human being. Evolution never proceeds in the simple straightforward way in which people are inclined to picture it. They imagine that time goes ever forward on and on to infinity. That is an altogether abstract conception. The truth is that time moves and turns in such a way that evolution is constantly reversed and runs back on itself. It is not only in space that we find movements in curves such as in a lemniscate but also in time.

During the Lemurian epoch the human being was at the crossing point of the lemniscate and that was the time when he implanted into himself the principle of electrical force. He traversed the return path in the Atlantean period and, in respect of certain forces, in the post-Atlantean period, and at about the end of the eighteenth and beginning of the nineteenth century arrived exactly at the point in the evolution of the cosmos at which he was in the old Lemurian age when he implanted into himself from the cosmos the principle of electricity. There you have the explanation of how it came about that Galvani discovered electricity at that particular time. Human beings always go back again in later times to what they experienced at an earlier stage. Life takes its course in cycles, in rhythms. In the middle of the materialistic age which had been developing since the fourteenth and fifteenth centuries, humankind was standing at that point in the cosmos through which it had passed long ago in the Lemurian epoch. And humankind as a whole at that point remembered the entry of electricity into the human being and as a result of this memory endowed the whole of civilization with electricity. The soul and spirit in the human being rediscovered what it had once experienced long ago.

[handwritten margin notes: ≈ 1800 AD ; 24,200 B.C.]

Truths like this must be clearly seen again, for it is only with truths like this that we shall escape decadence in the future.

Under the influence of the inspirations of which I have been speaking today, certain minds came upon such truths. For the fact that people embarked on such paths was the result of the fact that many and different currents work in human evolution. If, for example, what the Templars wanted to attain had been the sole influence working in history, quite a different evolution would have resulted for the human being. The fact that the other stream too—the mephistophelian one—has been mixed with it (the mephistophelian stream was of course also there from the beginning, but it was given new life by the destiny of the Templars) meant that the human being was introduced during this time to materialism just in the way that it actually happened. These mephistophelian-ahrimanic forces are needed in the evolution of humankind. And, as I said, certain great minds were led by the inspiration that comes from the Rosicrucian temples and has its source in the spiritual world to recognize this principle of which I have spoken here.

Do not imagine that a great poet, a really great poet who creates out of the spiritual world, composes his words in the superficial way that people often imagine they are at liberty to take them. No, a poet like Goethe, for instance, knows what is contained in and implied by the word. He knows that in the word we have something that carries with it the human being and with the human being the spirit, something that lets spirit resound through the person speaking. Person, did I say? Here we must remind ourselves that *persona* is a word that comes from the Greek for the mask that the actor wears and through which his voice sounds. *Personare* means to sound through. All this is closely connected with the evolution of the word. 'In the beginning was the Word, and the Word was with God, and the Word was God'. The word was not in the human being, nevertheless human personality is closely connected with it.

The whole of evolution, as we said, progresses not just through the work of good forces but others also. And a man like Goethe expressed in *Faust*, even though in part unconsciously but nevertheless through inspiration, notable and great truths. When the Lord is conversing with Mephistopheles in the 'Prologue in Heaven', he says finally to Mephistopheles that he has no objection to his work and influence. He recognizes and allows him his place in the evolution of the cosmos. It is owing to him that there are such things as temptations and influences that create evil. But then the Lord turns and directs his Word to the true and genuine sons of the gods who create progress in normal evolution and with whose work the work of the other stream is combined. And what does he say to these true sons of the gods?

But ye, true sons of Heaven, it is your duty
To take your joy in the living wealth of beauty.
The changing Essence which ever works and lives
Wall you around with love, serene, secure!
And that which floats in flickering appearance
Fix ye it firm in thoughts that must endure.
(Tr. Louis Macneice, Faber 1951)

The Lord gives to his sons the direct command to fix enduring thoughts in the places of the cosmos. Such an enduring thought was placed into the world when the principle of electricity was implanted into the human being and the human being was led back again to the enduring thought when he discovered the principle of electricity and implanted it into his materialistic civilization.

The thought expressed in the following lines is of immeasurable depth:

> The changing Essence which ever works and lives
> Wall you around with love, serene, secure!
> And that which floats in flickering appearance
> Fix ye it firm in thoughts that must endure.

And it represents a deep experience for the soul to feel the mystery of the 'thoughts that must endure'. For then we feel how in the world here and there the eternal stands at rest in the form of an enduring thought and we who belong to the world of movement are passing through what is being placed into 'that which floats in flickering appearance' as thoughts that must endure, as the beauty that weaves and works everlastingly and reveals itself in order that we may comprehend it when the right moment comes.

May a right moment also come for humankind in the near future, even as it is predestined to come if humankind is not to fall into decadence. May the human being understand that he has to pass through the next point which reverses materialism into its opposite, the point where the great thoughts of the spiritual world can ray into humankind. Preparation is now being made for this in those whose karma has allowed them to encounter spiritual science. And it will be the continually recurring task of spiritual science to turn its work in this direction. For to the materialistic age that has found the enduring thought which in its newest form Ahriman-Mephistopheles has placed into modern evolution must be added what can be experienced in passing through a spiritual enduring thought. Spiritual science must see to it that humankind does not fail to grasp this spiritual thought. Therefore also we must not cease in warning people repeatedly so that the moment of time for the comprehension of spiritual science does not slip by and is lost.

5. Sorat and the demise of the Templars (excerpt)

12 September 1924

This extract is part of a course given to the newly founded Christian Community priests and Rudolf Steiner clearly felt able to speak more freely about evil and the adversary power of the Sun Demon. The references to 'Arabism' should be taken in the context of his earlier lectures in 1918[49], where he describes more fully the role of Islam. The reason for this inclusion is the significance of 666 and its multiples, for as stated earlier, the Sun Demon's influence is not confined to a single year. That the effects of torture can lead to a kind of possession by adversary powers should make anyone who defends it reflect. The Templars condemned themselves thanks to this evil power and their unusual beliefs and practices became distorted and misunderstood in their inquisitors' minds. Steiner makes clear whom they really served, however, and it is possible that the Book of Revelation was part of their spiritual canon.

For the apocalyptist, then, the Sun Demon was particularly active around the year 666. He describes him in a way that allows any initiate to recognize him. All such spiritual beings, the Intelligences of the planets, Intelligences of the Sun, and the Demons of the planets and the Demons of the Sun have their key sign within the Mysteries where they are present during important ceremonies, and the Sun Demon has this sign:

The apocalyptist describes the Sun Demon as the two-horned beast. In the Latin era, during which Greek and Latin were joined together in the language of the Mysteries, the kind of reading that involved reading in numbers had already become external to some extent, but nevertheless, people did still read in numbers. The apocalyptist used the special mode of reading that was current in his day. He wrote the number 666 using Hebrew characters.

400	200	6	60
ת	ר	ו	ס
tau	resh	vai	samech

He wrote the characters by giving their number values, and he wrote them to be read from right to left. The consonants, to which the appropriate vowels must be added when speaking, give the name of the Demon that has this sign of the Sun Demon: Sorat. Sorat is the name of the Sun Demon at that time, and the apocalyptist describes this sign which we can easily recognize.[50] The apocalyptist sees everything that works against Christianity in this way—such as Arabism—as an outflowing of that spirituality which is represented by Sorat, the Sun Demon.

Dear friends, the number 666 was present on one occasion at the time when Arabism was flowing into Christianity in order to impress the seal of materialism on to western culture. But it was present for a second time after a further 666

1332
666
____
1998

1307
666
____
1973

Sorat and the demise of the Templars   107

years had passed, in 1332, in the fourteenth century. At that time once again the Beast rose up out of the waves of world events. To one whose vision is like that of the apocalyptist, world events appear as continuous waves of time-spans measuring 666 years. The Beast rises up to threaten Christianity in its search for true humanity; beasthood asserts itself against humanhood: Sorat stirs. In the fourteenth century we see Sorat, the adversary, rising up once again.

It was the time when, out of the deepest depths of soul much more than out of orientalism, the Order of the Knights Templar wanted to found a sun view of Christianity, a view of Christianity that looked up again to Christ as a Sun Being, as a cosmic being, a view that knew again about the spirits of the planets and stars, a view that knew how in cosmic events Intelligences from worlds that lie far apart from one another work together, not only the beings of one particular planet, a view that knew about the mighty oppositions that are brought about by such obstinate beings as Sorat, the Sun Demon, who is one of the most mighty demons in our system. What is at work in the materialism of human beings is, fundamentally, the demonic work of the Sun Demon.

It is of course difficult now to consider what might have become of European civilization if that powerful, that externally powerful Order of the Knights Templar—their riches were confiscated, as we know—had been able to achieve its goals. But in the hearts and souls of those who could not rest until the Order had been destroyed in 1312 and until Jacques de Molay had met his death in 1314, in the hearts of those who were the adversaries of the Christ who looked to the cosmos, in these hearts Sorat lived again, not least by making use of the Roman Church's attitude of mind at that time to bring about the death of the Templars. The appearance of Sorat was more visible than it had been the previous time, and the demise of the Templars is shrouded in a stupendous secret. When you can see into what went on in the souls of the Templars while they were being tortured you can gain some idea of how what lived in their visions was instigated by Sorat. As a result they slandered themselves, providing their enemies with a cheap indictment through what they themselves uttered. People were confronted with the terrible spectacle of seeing individuals being unable to speak about what they genuinely represented, while different spirits from among the cohorts of Sorat spoke through them instead, accusing the Order of the most disgusting things out of the mouths of its own adherents.

The number 666 has twice been fulfilled. And now the time has come in the spiritual world when Sorat and the other opposing demons are preparing to prevent the Sun Principle from entering into the earth. Michael, on the other hand, preparing for his new regency, is fighting with his hosts for this entry of the Sun Principle. Michael was regent of the earth before the time of the Mystery of Golgotha, around the time of Alexander. The other archangels then in turn took over from him: Oriphiel, Anael, Zachariel, Raphael, Gabriel. Since the last third of the nineteenth century he has again been regent of the earth in order to continue working in his way for Christ, for whom he worked until his previous regency ended, approximately until the end of Alexander's rule. Michael is on the earth once again, this time in order to serve here on earth the preparation for Christ and for the deeper comprehension of the Christ-Impulse.

As time has gone on I have spoken here and in various other places about how Christianity has been introduced spiritually through Michael. I mentioned one aspect of this two days ago when I spoke in a lecture[51] about Michael's regency in the time of Aristotle and Alexander, during which a genuinely Christian impulse was already introduced, and when I also pointed to the year 869 in which a kind of supersensory Council took place. This continued further. And at the beginning of the new era, when the consciousness soul is beginning to take effect, we now have—if we look up to spiritual events belonging to earthly humanity and running parallel with earthly events—the wonderful sight of a supersensory school with Michael as its teacher. Those who were to work towards a real development of Christianity, souls not at the moment incarnated on the earth, and also other spiritual beings, were gathered in great numbers around Michael, from the fourteenth to the sixteenth century, as though in a great, supersensory school in which those souls were being prepared who were to appear on earth at the beginning of the twentieth century during Michael's regency. When we look at what was being prepared there we find that it was the anthroposophical world view, which wants to work for this evolution.

From what the ancient Mystery wisdom saw, and through the prophetic sight of future Mystery wisdom, we gather that human beings who take in what we call the inner Christianity, the spiritualized Christianity, those who look to the Genius of the Sun with regard to Christ—these individuals will experience an acceleration of their evolution and reappear on the earth again at the end of the twentieth century. Dear friends, everything we are able to do now in our time by way of taking in the spirituality of these teachings is of great significance, for we are doing it for the human beings who are, *sub specie aeternitatis*, alive at this time. It is a preparation for what is to take place at the end of the century, initially in the form of great, all-embracing, intense deeds of the spirit, after a great deal will have happened that is inimical to a spiritualization of modern civilization. The great revolutions that came about in Europe as a result of the Crusades belonged

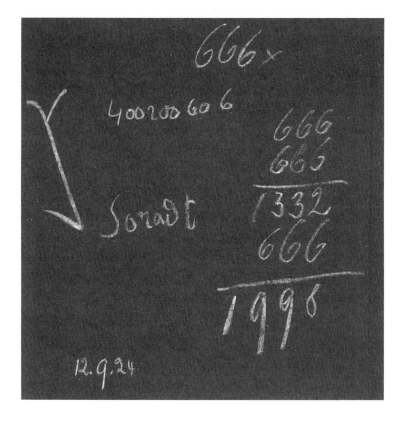

under the sign of the second occurrence of the number 666. This fact found its expression in the demise of the Templars. Sorat continues to work on and on against the forces coming from the Genius of the Sun that are battling for a genuine Christianity.

Before us lies the time of the third number 666: 1998. At the end of this century the time will come when Sorat will once again raise his head most strongly out of the waves of evolution to become the adversary of that appearance of Christ which those who have been prepared for it will already experience during the first half of the twentieth century when the Etheric Christ becomes visible. Only two-thirds of the century have still to run before Sorat once again raises his head most mightily.

During the first 666, dear friends, Sorat was still hidden away inside the evolutionary process of events; he was not seen in any external form, for he lived within the deeds of Arabism, and initiates were able to see him. When the second 666 years had passed he showed himself in the thinking and feeling of the tortured Templars. And before this century is out he will show himself by making his appearance in many humans as the being by whom they are possessed. Human beings will appear of whom it will be impossible to believe that they are real human beings. They will even develop externally in a peculiar manner, for outwardly they will have intense, strong dispositions with savage features and furious destructiveness in their emotions. Their faces will be like the faces of beasts. The Sorat human beings will be recognizable by their external appearance; in a terrible way they will not only scoff at everything but also oppose and want to push into the pool of filth anything that is spiritual. This will be experienced, for example, in the way something that is at present concentrated into a small space in seed form as today's Bolshevism will become incorporated into the whole of human evolution on earth. — in USA

That is why it is so important that all who are capable of doing so should strive for spirituality. What is inimical to spirituality will be there anyway, for it works not through freedom but under determinism. This determinism has already decreed that at the end of this century Sorat will be on the loose again, so that the intention to sweep away anything spiritual will be deep-seated in large numbers of earthly souls, just as the apocalyptist has foreseen in the beast-like countenance and the beast-like strength that will underlie the deeds of the adversary against the spiritual. Even today the rage against spiritual things is already immense. Yet it is still only in its very early infancy.

All this was foreseen by the apocalyptist. He saw the true unfolding of Christianity as a matter connected with the Sun, but he also foresaw how terrible would be the unfolding of the Sun Demon. All this appeared before him. The entry of Michael into the spiritual evolution of humanity at the end of the nineteenth century, and the appearance of the Etheric Christ during the first half of the twentieth century are events that will be followed by the arrival of the Sun Demon before this century comes to an end. In this Michael age of ours, especially if we want to work in the realm of theology and religion, we have every reason to learn above all from the Book of Revelation how to think and feel in an apocalyptic way, how not to remain stuck in what are merely external facts but how to rise up to the spiritual impulses that lie behind them.

The trail is being blazed for the entry of the demons, the adherents of the great Demon Sorat. To gain an idea of this you only need to speak to people who understand something of what led to the World War. It is fair to say that of the approximately forty people who are guilty of causing that war, almost all were in a state of lowered consciousness at the moment when it broke out. Such a state of consciousness is always a way in for ahrimanic demonic powers, and one of the greatest of these demons is Sorat. Such are the attempts Sorat is making to gain at least temporary access to the consciousness of human beings in order to bring about calamity and confusion. Not the World War itself, but what followed it and what is even more terrible and what will become more terrible still—for example the present state in which Russia finds herself—this is what the Sorat spirits who invade human souls are aiming at.

We must be aware of the fact that this is so. For in times when there was true spirituality on the earth, what did it mean to work as a priest? It has always meant, dear friends, that one worked not only within the sphere of earthly events but also in full consciousness of how one stands in the spiritual world, in intercourse with the divine world. This and no other was the spirit in which the apocalyptist wrote his Book of Revelation. Someone who wants to lead human beings into the spirit must himself be able to see into the spirit. Every age has to do this in its own way. Look at the inner laws according to which—although perhaps somewhat alienated from the spirit—the sequence of Egyptian pharaohs appears to be so logical. We can glean from this that the succession of pharaohs was indeed not arbitrary. Ancient scriptures told which task each pharaoh following on the previous one must regard as his specific obligation and that the impulse for the formulation of that obligation emerged from what later came to be called the Hermetic revelation, the revelation of Hermes. I do not mean the Hermetic revelation we know today in a somewhat bowdlerized version, but the ancient Hermes wisdom that also belongs to the great Mysteries in which one spoke of the revelation as being three times holy: a revelation of the Father, a revelation of the Son, a revelation of the Holy Spirit. All this points to the fact that priestly work everywhere meant working out of the spirit into the material world; this is what priesthood was always understood to signify.

This is what the impulse of priesthood must once again become, now that the period of time is over when it was not felt to be true that one can work out of the spiritual world. With the culture and education we have today, which in the era of the consciousness soul has gradually come to take on materialistic forms in every field, people are very far from being able to comprehend such a thing as the mystery of the transubstantiation and with this the spiritual mysteries of Christianity. For individual priests today, contemporary education makes it seem like a kind of untruth to speak of the profound contents of the Mysteries that are connected with the transubstantiation. Hence the rationalistic discussions about transubstantiation that began at the time of the second attack by Sorat and continue today up to the time of the third attack. There is absolutely no point in taking the Book of

Revelation as something about which commentaries can be written. The only meaningful thing to do is to learn through the Book of Revelation how to become an apocalyptist oneself, and in becoming an apocalyptist to get to understand one's own time so well that the impulses of that time become the impulses of one's own work.

As a human being of the present time and as a priest one can enter into this by looking directly at the beginning of the Michael age in the 1870s, at the appearance of Christ in the first half of the twentieth century, and at the threatening rise of Sorat and his adherents at the end of the twentieth century. As human beings who understand these things and know how to interpret the signs of the times, let us arrange our lives in accordance with these three mysteries of our time: the mystery of Michael, the mystery of Christ, and the mystery of Sorat. If we do this, we shall work in the right way in the field to which our karma has led us, and so will the priest in his priestly field. We shall continue from here tomorrow.

6. Templar beliefs

22 May 1905

We return to an earlier lecture here in order to gain some understanding of the Templars' spiritual beliefs which were to cause such opposition. The context of this is Freemasonry and the Lodge which Steiner took over in order to link on to this spiritual stream by means of his own ritual work.[52]

It becomes clear from other lectures in the volume and the lessons which he gave to members of this part of his first esoteric school, that there was a branch of Freemasonry which dates back to the time of St Mark who founded the rite of Misraim together with Ormus, his convert, a priest of the Isis mysteries. Although this Egyptian origin is sometimes denied by Masonic historians, there are others who have alluded to it. The mystery knowledge developed there was to pass to the Templars in the Holy Land. For a possible account of how this came about, see the recent work The Sion Revelation,[53] *p. 306.*

This lecture neatly summarizes the main Templar beliefs, the sacred geometry, reverence for John the Baptist and the divine feminine, the meaning of the 'Temple'. Steiner gives some indications of the ritual referred to in the 'secret statutes'—denial of the Cross, venerating a symbolic Head, and it is thus one of the most revealing of his statements about the Order. Dante's connection with the Order has been explored by Manfred Schmidt-Brabant in the publication Denker, Heilige, Ketzer.[54]

A few more reflections on the lost temple. We must regard Solomon's Temple as the greatest symbol. Now the point is to understand this symbol. You know the course of events from the Bible, how it began. In this case, we are not dealing with mere symbols but in fact with outward realities in which, however, a profound world-historic symbolism finds its expression at the same time. And those who built the temple were aware of what it was meant to express.

Let us consider why the temple was built. And you will see that each word in the Bible's account of it[55] is a deeply significant symbol. In this you need only consider in what period the building was erected. Let us particularly recall the biblical explanation for what the temple was to be. Yahveh addressed this explanation to David: 'A house for My Name'—that is, a house for the name Yahveh. And now let us make clear what the name Yahveh signifies.

Ancient Judaism became quite clear, at a particular time, about the holiness of the name Yahveh. What does it mean? A child learns at a certain moment in its life to use the word 'I'. Before that, it regards itself as a thing. Just as it gives names to other things, so it even calls itself by an objective name. Only later does it learn to use the word 'I'. The moment in the lives of great personalities when they first experience their own 'I', when they first become aware of themselves, is charged with significance. Jean Paul recounts the following incident.[56] As a small boy he was once standing in a barn in a farmyard. At that moment he first experienced his own 'I'. And so serene and solemn was this instant for him, that he said of it, 'I then looked into my innermost soul as into the Holy of Holies'.

Humankind has developed through many epochs and everyone conceived themselves in this objective way up to

Atlantean times; only during the Atlantean epoch did the human being develop to the stage where he could say 'I' to himself. The ancient Hebrews included this in their doctrines.

Human beings have passed through the kingdoms of nature. Ego consciousness rose in them last of all. The astral, etheric and physical bodies and the ego together form the Pythagorean square. And Judaism added the divine ego to it which descends from above, in contrast to the ego from below. Thus a pentagon has been made out of the square. This was how Judaism experienced the Lord God of its people and it was therefore a sacred thing to utter the 'Name'. Whereas other names, such as 'Elohim' or 'Adonai', came increasingly into use, only the anointed priest in the Holy of Holies was allowed to utter the name 'Yahveh'.[57] It was in the time of Solomon that ancient Judaism came to the holiness of the name Yahveh, to this 'I' which can dwell in the human being. We must take Jehovah's challenge to human beings as something that sought to have the human being himself made into a temple of the most holy God. Now we have gained a new conception of the Godhead, namely this: the God which is hidden in the human being's breast, in the deepest holiness of the human being's self, must be changed into a moral God. The human body is thus turned into a great symbol of the Inner Sanctuary.

And now an outward symbol had to be erected as the human being is God's temple. The temple had to be a symbol, illustrating the human being's own body. Therefore builders were sent for—Hiram-Abiff—who understood the practical arts that could transform the human being himself

into a god. Two images in the Bible relate to this: one is
Noah's Ark and the other is the Temple of Solomon.[58] In
one way both are the same, yet they also have to be distinguished.

Noah's Ark was built to preserve humankind for the
present stage of human existence. Before Noah, human
beings lived in the Atlantean and Lemurian epochs. At that
time he had not built the ship which was to carry him across
the waters of the astral world into earthly existence. The
human being came by the waters of the astral world and
Noah's Ark carried him over. The Ark represents the con-
struction built by unconscious divine forces. From the
measurements given, its proportions correspond to those of
the human body and also those of Solomon's Temple.[59]

The human being has developed beyond Noah's Ark and
now he has to surround his higher self with a house created
by his own spirit, by his own wisdom, by the wisdom of
Solomon.

We enter the Temple of Solomon. The door itself is
characteristic. The square used to function as an old symbol.
Humankind has now progressed from the stage of four-
foldness to that of fivefoldness, as the five-membered human
being who has become conscious of his own higher self. The
inner divine temple is so formed as to enclose the fivefold
human being. The square is holy. The door, the roof and the
side pillars together form a pentagon.[60, 61] When the human
being awakens from his fourfold state, that is, when he enters
his inner being—the inner sanctuary is the most important
part of the temple—he sees a kind of altar. We perceive two
cherubim which hover like two guardian spirits over the Ark

of the Covenant, the Holy of Holies, for the fifth principle [of the human being's being] which has not yet descended to earth must be guarded by the two higher beings buddhi and manas. Thus the human being enters the stage of manas development.

The whole inner sanctuary is covered in gold because gold has always been the symbol of wisdom. Now wisdom enters the manas stage. We find palm leaves as the symbol of peace. That represents a particular epoch of humanity and is inserted here as something that only came to expression later in Christianity. The Temple leaders guarded this within themselves, in this way expressing something intended for later developments.

Later, in the Middle Ages, the idea of Solomon's Temple was revived again in the Knights Templar who sought to introduce the temple-thinking in the West. But the Knights Templar were misunderstood at that time (for example, the trial of Jacques [de] Molay, their Grand Master). If we wish to understand the Templars, we must look deeply into human history. What the Templars were accused of at their trial rests entirely on a major misunderstanding. The Knights Templar said at the time: 'Everything we have experienced so far is a preparation for what the redeemer wishes. For Christianity', they continued, 'has a future, new task. And we have the task of preparing the various sects of the Middle Ages and humanity generally for a future in which Christianity will emerge into new clarity as the redeemer actually intended that it should. We saw Christianity rise in the fourth cultural epoch; it will develop further in the fifth, but only in the sixth will it celebrate the glory of its resurrection. We have to prepare for that. We must guide human souls in such a way that a genuine, true and pure Christianity may come to expression in which the Name of the Most High may find its dwelling place'.

Jerusalem was to be its centre and from there the secret concerning the relationship of the human being to the Christ should stream out all over the world. What was represented symbolically by the temple should become a living reality. It was said of the Templars, and this was an accusation against them, that they had instituted a kind of star-worship or, similarly, a sun-worship. However, a great mystery lies behind this. The sacrament of the Mass was originally nothing else but a great mystery. Mass fell into two parts: the so-called Minor Mass, in which all were allowed to take part; and when that had ended and the main body [of the congregation] had gone away, there followed the High Mass which was intended only for those who wished to undergo occult training, to embark on the 'Path'. In this High Mass the reciting of the Apostolic Creed took place first. Then was expounded the development of Christianity throughout the world and how it was connected with the great march of world evolution.

The conditions on earth were not always the same as today. The earth was once joined to the sun and the moon. The sun separated itself, as it were, and then shone upon the earth from outside. Later, the moon split away. Thus, in earlier times, the earth was quite a different kind of dwelling place for human beings. The human being was quite different physically at that time. But when the sun and the moon split off from the earth, the whole of the human being's life underwent a change. Birth and death took place for the first time, human beings reincarnated for the first time, and for the first time the ego of the human being, the individuality, descended into the physical body to reincarnate in continuous succession. One day that will cease again. The earth will again become joined to the sun and then human beings will be able to pass through their further evolution on the sun. Thus we have a specific series of steps according to which the sun and human beings move together. Such things are connected with the progress of the sun across the vault of heaven.

Now everything that happens in the world is briefly recapitulated in the following stages. Everything has been repeated, including the evolution of the global stages in the first, second and third great epochs. It came about, then, that human beings descended into reincarnation. The sun split away [from the earth] during the time of transition from the second to the third great epoch, the moon became separated during the third epoch [Lemuria]. Now the earth is developing from the third to the sixth epoch when the sun will again be joined to the earth. Then a new epoch will start in which human beings will have attained a much higher stage and will no longer incarnate.

This teaching concerning the course of evolution came into the world through religion in the shape of the story of Noah's Ark. This teaching foreshadowed what was to happen in the future. The union of the sun with the earth is foreshadowed in the appearance of Christ on earth. It is always so with such teachings. For a time what happens is a repetition of the past, then the teaching begins to be a prefiguring of the future. Each individual cultural epoch, as it relates to the evolution of consciousness for each nation, is connected with the progression of the sun through the zodiac.

You know that the time of transition from the third to the fourth cultural epoch was represented by the sign of the Ram or Lamb. The Babylonian-Assyrian epoch gathered together in the sign of the Bull all that was important for its time. The previous Persian age was characterized by the sign of the Twins. And if we go still further into the past we would come to the sign of the Crab for Sanskrit culture. This epoch, in which the sun was in Cancer at the time of the spring equinox, was a turning-point for humanity. Atlantis had been submerged and the first cultural epoch of the fifth great epoch had begun. This turning-point was denoted by the Crab. The next cultural epoch similarly begins with the transition of the sun into the sign of the Twins. A further stage of history leads us over into the culture of Asia Minor and Egypt as the sun passes into the sign of the Bull. And as the sun continues its course through the zodiac the fourth cultural epoch begins which is connected in Greek legend with the Ram or Lamb (the saga of Jason and the search for the Golden Fleece). And Christ himself was later on in early Christian times represented by the Lamb. He called himself the Lamb.

We have traced the time from the first to the fourth cultural epoch.[62] The sun proceeds through the heavens, and now we enter the sign of the Fishes where we are ourselves at a critical point. Then [in the future], in the time of the sixth epoch, the time will arrive when human beings will have become so inwardly purified that they themselves become a temple for the divine. At that time the sun will enter the sign of Aquarius. Thus the sun, which is really only the external expression of our spiritual life, progresses in heavenly space. When the sun enters the sign of Aquarius at the spring equinox, it will then be understood completely clearly for the first time.

Thus proceeded the High Mass from which all the uninitiated were excluded. It was made clear to those who remained that Christianity, which began as a seed, would in the future bear something quite different as fruit and that the name Aquarius referred to John [the Baptist] who scatters Christianity as a seed, as if with a grain of mustard seed. Aquarius or the Water Carrier points to the same person as John who baptized with water in order to prepare humankind to receive the Christian baptism of fire. The fact of the coming of a 'John/Aquarius' who will first confirm the old John and then announce a Christ who will renew the temple once the great point of time arrives when Christ will again speak to humanity—this was taught in the depths of the Templar Mysteries, so that the event should be understood.

Moreover, the Templars said: Today we live at a point in time when human beings are not yet ripe for understanding the great teachings; we still have to prepare them for the Baptist, John, who baptizes with water. The cross was held up before the would-be Templar and he was told: You must deny the cross now so as to understand it later; first become a Peter, first deny the scriptures, like Peter the Rock who denied the Lord. That was imparted to the aspirant Templar as a preliminary training.

People generally understand so little of all this that even

the letters on the cross are not interpreted correctly. Plato said of it that the world soul is crucified on the world body.[63] The cross symbolizes the four elements. The plant, animal and human kingdoms are built out of these four elements. On the cross is written: JAM = water = *James*; NOUR = fire, which refers to *Jesus* himself; RUACH = air, the symbol for *John*; and the fourth JABESCHAH = earth or rock, for *Peter*.

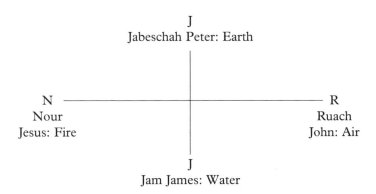

J
Jabeschah Peter: Earth

N —————————————— R
Nour   Ruach
Jesus: Fire   John: Air

J
Jam James: Water

Thus there stands on the cross what is expressed in the names of the [three] apostles [and Jesus], while the one name INRI denotes Christ himself. 'Earth' is the place where Christianity itself must at first be brought, to that temple to which the human being himself has brought himself so as to be a sheath for what is higher. But this temple ... [Gap in text][64]

The cock, which is the symbol for both the human being's higher and lower selves, 'crows twice' [Mark 14:30]. The cock crows for the first time when the human being descends [to earth] and becomes materialized in physical substance; it crows for the second time when the human being rises again, when he has learnt to understand Christ, when Aquarius appears. That will be in the sixth cultural epoch. Then the human being will understand spiritually what he should become. The ego will have attained a certain stage then, when what Solomon's Temple stands for will be reality in the highest sense, when the human being himself is a temple for Yahveh.

Before that, however, the human being still has to undergo three stages of purification. The ego is in a threefold sheath: firstly, in the astral body; secondly, in the etheric body; thirdly in the physical body. When we are in the astral body, we deny the divine ego for the first time, we do so for the second time in the etheric body, and for the third time in the physical body. The first crow of the cock is threefold denial through the threefold sheath of the human being. And when he has then passed through the three bodies, when the ego discovers in Christ its greatest symbolical realization, then the cock crows for the second time.

None of the Templars who were put under torture at that time were able to convey these profound thoughts to their judges—this struggle to raise oneself up to a proper understanding of Christ, first passing through the stage of Peter. These were thoughts which raised them to an actual understanding of the Christ.

At the outset, the Templars were in a position as if they had abjured the cross. After all of this had been made clear to the Templar, he was shown a symbolical figure of the Divine Being in the form of a venerable man with a long beard (symbolizing the Father). When human beings have developed and have come to receive in the Master a leader from among themselves, when those are there who are able to lead humanity, then, as the Word of the guiding Father, there will stand before men the Master who leads human beings to the comprehension of Christ.

And then it was said to the Templars: When you have understood all this, you will be ripe for joining in building the great temple of the earth; you must co-operate in this way, so arrange everything that this great building becomes a dwelling place for our true deeper selves, for our inner Ark of the Covenant.

If we survey all this, we find images having great significance. And he in whose soul these images come alive will become more and more fit to become a disciple of those great Masters who are preparing the building of the temple of humankind. For such great concepts work powerfully in our souls, so that we thereby undergo purification, so that we are led to abounding life in the spirit.

We find the same medieval tendency as manifested in the Knights Templar in two Round Tables as well, that of King Arthur and that of the Holy Grail.[25] In King Arthur's Round Table can be found the ancient universality, whereas the spirituality proper to Christian knighthood had to be prepared in those who guarded the Mystery of the Holy Grail. It is remarkable how calmly and tranquilly medieval people contemplated the developing power (fruit) and outward form of Christianity.

When you follow the teaching of the Templars, there at the heart of it is a kind of reverence for something of a feminine nature. This femininity was known as the Divine Sophia, the Heavenly Wisdom. Manas is the fifth principle, the spiritual self of the human being, that must be developed and for which a temple must be built. And, just as the pentagon at the entrance to Solomon's Temple characterizes the fivefold human being, this female principle similarly typifies the wisdom of the Middle Ages. This wisdom is exactly what Dante sought to personify in his Beatrice. Only from this viewpoint can Dante's Divine Comedy [*Divina Commedia*] be understood. Hence you find Dante,[54] too, using the same symbols as those which find expression in the Templars, the Christian knights, the Knights of the Grail, and so on. Everything that is to happen [in the future] was indeed long since prepared for by the great initiates, who foretell future events, in the same way as in the Apocalypse, so that souls will be prepared for these events.

According to legend, there were two different currents when humanity came to the earth. The Children of Cain, whom one of the Elohim begat through Eve, the Children of the Earth, in whom we find the great arts and external sciences—that is one of the currents. It was banished, but is however to be sanctified by Christianity when the fifth principle comes into the world. The other current is that of the Children of God who have led human beings towards an understanding of the fifth principle. They are the ones that Adam created. Now the Sons of Cain were called upon to create an outer sheath, to contain what the Sons of God, the Abel-Seth Children, created.

In the Ark of the Covenant lies concealed the Holy Name of Yahveh. However, what is needed to transform the world, to create the sheath for the Holy of Holies, must be accomplished again through the Sons of Cain. God created the human being's physical body, into which human being's ego

works, at first destroying this temple. The human being can
only be rescued if he first builds the house to carry him across
the waters of the emotions—if he builds Noah's Ark for
himself. This house must set the human being on his feet
again. Now those who came into the world as the Children of
Cain are building the outward part, and what the Children of
God have brought to it is building the inner part.

These two streams were already current when our race
began ... [Gap][65]

So we shall only understand theosophy when we look upon
it as a testament laying the foundations for what the Temple
of Solomon denotes and for what the future holds in store.
We have to prepare for the New Covenant, in place of the
Old Covenant. The old one is the Covenant of the creating
God, in which God is at work on the temple of humankind.
The New Covenant is the one in which the human being
himself surrounds the divine with the temple of wisdom,
when he restores it, so that this 'I' will find a sanctuary on this
earth when it is resurrected out of matter, set free.

Such is the profundity of the symbols, and such was the
instruction that the Templars wanted to be allowed to confer
upon humankind. The Rosicrucians are none other than the
successors to the Order of the Templars, wanting nothing
else than the Templars did, which is also what theosophy
desires: they are all at work on the great temple of humanity.

7. The Soul's Probation (Four Mystery Plays) (excerpts)

Included here are extracts from the medieval scenes in the second Mystery Drama. Rudolf Steiner was attempting to show the karma in a former life of Capesius, the twentieth-century historian, who represents a perplexed modern soul 'trapped in darkness' and unable to find his true bearings, portrayed in these scenes as the First Preceptor.

Although Steiner does not actually name the 'Mystic Order' as the Knights Templar, it is perfectly clear from the text that he has it in mind. Moreover the scenes are set in a specific location: Castle Lockenhaus in the Burgenland,[66] eastern Austria, close to where he grew up. It was a Templar castle which held out for some years after the arrests in France but which finally succumbed. He would have been familiar with local stories of a secret passage and the betrayal of the Knights by a fervently Catholic peasant. The scenes take place following the death of Jacques de Molay, the last Grand Master of the Order.

In these scenes the local Grand Master converses with fellow Knights on the deeper beliefs of the Order, the understanding of Christ as a cosmic being from the sun sphere who descended to earth in the body of Jesus at the baptism, reincarnation, the future redemption of evil, thus setting them firmly in their Gnostic-Manichaean stream. In a further scene, a Dominican monk enters the castle to press a claim that the land on which the Knights have developed a mine really belongs to the Church. The monk is overwhelmed by his horror at the 'heresy' around him, but the spirit of his teacher Benedictus comes to him, who is most likely a manifestation of the great Dominican Thomas Aquinas. He defends the Order and tries to explain its true aims to the monk. The self-sacrificing nature of its real purpose comes across very clearly.

They are framed by two scenes in which some local peasants speak both for and against the Knights. Some object to the Knights having granted asylum to a Jew who is skilled in medicine. In the final scene, the hostile peasants declare their intention to betray the Order.

Scenes Six, Seven, Eight and Nine take place during the first third of the fourteenth century.

SCENE SIX

> *A forest glade. In the background a high cliff on which stands a castle. A summer evening. Peasants pass through the glade and speak together as they pause along the way.*

FIRST PEASANT   See here, the wicked Jew;
he will not dare
to take the same path as we,
for he might hear such things as burn his
     ears.

SECOND PEASANT

We should show him for good and all
we shall no longer tolerate his boldness,
sneaking across the border into our quiet
     homeland!

FIRST WOMAN   He is protected by the lords
who live there in the castle.
Not one of us is given entrance;

the Jew they readily admit. He does
whatever they would have him do.

THIRD PEASANT 'Tis hard to know who's serving God,
who's serving Hell.
We should be thankful to our knights;
they give us bread as well as work.
Where should we be without them?

SECOND WOMAN

Now I must say a good word for the Jew.
He freed me of my cruel sickness
by his own remedies.
He was so kind and good beside.
He's done the same for many others, too.

THIRD WOMAN A monk, however, has divulged to me
that devilish are the means by which he
    heals.
Be well on guard against his poison.
'Tis said to change within the body,
and offer entrance to all sins.

FOURTH PEASANT

The men who serve the knights
combat our ancient customs.
They say the Jew knows much
that good and blessing brings,
but will be rightly valued
only in days to come.

FIFTH PEASANT   New and better times are soon in store:
I can foresee them in the spirit
for pictures from the soul show things
my body's eyes cannot behold.
The knights are willing
to bring all this about for us.

FOURTH WOMAN
It's to the church we owe our loyalty;
it saves our souls from devil pictures,
from death and from the pangs of hell.
The monks do warn us of the knights
and of the sorcerer, the Jew.

FIFTH WOMAN   We shall not bear this yoke much longer
imposed upon our patience by the knights.
The castle will soon lie in ruins;
a vision in a dream revealed all this to me.

SIXTH WOMAN   The fear of heavy sin torments me
when I listen to the people say
the knights are plotting to destroy us.
I see but good in all that comes from them.
I needs must call them Christian too.

SIXTH PEASANT   How men will think in days to come,
let us leave that to those
who shall live after us.
The knights are using us as tools
to work their devil's arts
with which they fight
what's truly Christian.

When they are driven out,
we shall be free of their control
and live our lives as we shall choose,
here in our native land.

★   ★   ★

SCENE SEVEN

*A room within the castle which in Scene Six was viewed from
outside. It is decorated with symbols of a Mystic Brotherhood.
First, the Knights are shown during a meeting, then the Monk
with one of the Knights; later there appears the Spirit of Benedictus, who has died fifty years earlier. The Grand Master with
four Knights are gathered about a long table.*

GRAND MASTER   You have become companions to me
in search of mankind's future goals.
We are directed by our Order's precepts
to bring these aims from spirit regions
into the realm of earth activity.
So loyally stand by me now
within this hour of grave concern.
Our venerable leader fell[67]
a victim to those powers of darkness
which draw their strength from evil
and yet promote the plan of wisdom
by opposition's force. This plan
seeks to convert the evil into good.
But since our leader's death,
our earthly strivings are in vain.

Our enemies have overthrown already
many a castle of our brotherhood,
and fighting, many of our valiant brothers
have followed the great master
into the bright realms of eternity.
For us, too, the hour is close at hand
when these protecting walls must fall.
Our enemies are spying out the means
by which they can take hold of our
   possessions.
These we've surely not acquired for profit,
but as a means to gather round us people
into whose souls we can implant
seeds for the future.
These seeds will ripen in their souls
when out of spirit realms they find their
   way
into a later life on earth.

FIRST MASTER OF CEREMONY

Our Order must endure whatever dark
   design
our destiny has yet in store.
This, one can understand.
But that in perishing, our whole
   community
must sweep with it
so many brothers' individual lives,
seems an injustice in the light of cosmic
   laws.

My lips will not complain,
for manfully our brothers died;
but still my soul desires to understand
the sacrifice required of a man
united with a group
when powers of destiny have doomed
that group to its destruction.

GRAND MASTER The individual's separate life
is linked most wisely with the cosmic plan.
Among our brothers one proves often able
to serve our Order with his spirit forces
although his life is not unblemished.
His erring course of heart and mind will
    find
atonement through the sufferings
he has to bear in service to the whole.
On him who bears no guilt from his own
    deeds
yet has to walk the thorny path
marked out by karma for our Order,
pain will bestow new strength
to raise himself to higher life.

FIRST MASTER OF CEREMONY

Then does our Order tolerate within
    itself[68]
men also, lacking purity of soul,
who consecrate themselves to its high
    goals?

GRAND MASTER The one who works devotedly for lofty
                 aims,
             he weighs the good alone in souls of men
             and he allows the bad to find atonement
             within the course of cosmic justice.
             I've summoned you, my brothers,
             in these our days of grief
             in order to recall to you with earnest words,
             that it behoves us joyfully to die—
             for goals to which we pledged ourselves
             to dedicate our lives.
             In the truest sense you are my brothers
             when in your souls resound courageously
             our Order's words of consecration:
             'The separate life and being must be
                 sacrificed
             by him who would set eyes on spirit goals
             through sense-world revelation;
             who would, with courage, dare
             to pour into his individual will
             the spirit's power of will'.

FIRST PRECEPTOR

             Most worthy master, if you would test
             the hearts of all our brothers,
             in clearest echo will resound to you
             those words of consecration.
             But we would hear from your own lips
             how to construe the fact
             that with our lands and lives,

the enemy robs us of souls as well
whom with our love we nurtured.
For every day makes it more clear
our people will surrender to the victors
not only through compulsion
but through the hate our foes have taught
    them
against the spirit path which we have
    shown.

GRAND MASTER What we have planted in their souls
indeed may for the present die.
But those who breathed our spirit light
will come again, and then bestow
upon the world what we intended in our
    work.
Thus to my spirit from realms of death
our mighty leader often speaks,
when I descend in hours of silence
into my inner depths,
and forces then awaken,
to hold me in the spirit land.
I feel the presence of our leader then
and hear his words
as often I have heard them
in earthly life.
He does not speak of our work's ending,
but of fulfilment of our goals
in later days on earth.

                         ★   ★   ★

MONK (*alone*)	O that my office forces me to enter
	the hall of this most hateful Order.
	On every side my eye encounters
	these devilish designs and sinful images.
	An agonizing horror grips me . . .
	It's crackling—O it's rumbling through the
	    hall;
	I feel how evil powers want to encircle
	    me . . .
	
	As I am not aware of any sin,
	I bid defiance to the adversaries
	
	The horror grows . . .
	O . . .
	
	(*The Spirit of Benedictus appears.*)
	
	All good spirits, stand by me now!

BENEDICTUS	Take heed, my son! I could draw near you frequently when fervent prayer transported you to spirit worlds. So hear with courage also in this hour what you must bring to clear cognition, if spirit light in place of darkness should now hold sway within your soul.
MONK	When I begged earnestly for clarity in moments of distress and my devoted prayer was granted hearing in the spirit land,

then you appeared to me, great master,
who was the glory of our Order
in days you lived on earth.
You spoke to me from higher realms,
illumining my sense
and strengthening my power.
My soul's eye could behold you,
my spirit ear could hear you.
And now devoutly in this hour
I'll listen to the revelation
which flows from you into my soul.

BENEDICTUS   You find yourself within that Order's
                  house
which you accuse of evil heresy.
It seems to hate all that we love
and to revere what we deem sin.
Our brothers hold themselves obliged to
                  hasten
the downfall of this sin against the spirit.
In this they are supported
by words which formerly I spoke on earth.
They do not dream
these very words can only be renewed
if they are nurtured for their further growth
by those who are successors in my work.
So let arise within your soul
what I once thought in former days on
                  earth,
but now what it must be

in view of a new age.
The Order here accepts its goals
from occult heights.
Look on it in that light
as I myself would do
if I could walk among you actively
within an earthly body.
This Order strives towards highest goals.
And those who dedicate themselves to it
divine already future times on earth.
Their leaders see with a prophetic eye
the fruits that ripen in a later age.
Both science and men's way of life
will change in form and aim.
This Order, whose persecution you
    support,
now feels impelled to undertake
the deeds which serve this change.
And only when our brothers' aims
unite for peaceful purposes
with those the heretics pursue,
can good in earthly progress blossom forth.

MONK   The admonition you have found me
             worthy of,
         how can I follow it?
         It deviates most forcefully from all
         that in the past seemed right to me.

SCENE EIGHT

> (*The two Masters of Ceremony enter the hall.*)

FIRST MASTER OF CEREMONY

> I must confess quite frankly, my dear
> brother,
> that the forbearance of our master seems to
> me
> incomprehensible when I must see
> the great injustice of our enemies.
> They do not want to know about our
> teachings
> but paint them frighteningly to people
> as heresy and as the devil's work.
>
> . . .

SECOND MASTER OF CEREMONY

> Among them many follow
> Christ's example honestly.
> The deepest meaning of our teachings
> remains, however, sealed for those
> who hear them only with an outer ear.
> My brother, remember how reluctantly,
> with inner opposition, you grew willing
> to listen to the Spirit Word.
> From what our masters have revealed we
> know
> how, through the light of spirit, future men
> will see the lofty Being of the Sun
> Who lived but once within an earthly body.

With joy we can believe the revelation
because we follow trustfully our leaders.
But recently the man that we acknowledge
our Order's head, spoke these important
   words:
'Your souls must gradually mature
if you'd behold prophetically
what will reveal itself to men in future.
But do not think', he also said,
'that after your first soul probation
this premonition will appear to you.
For even when you have the certainty
of men's return to life on earth,
you'll have to face the second test
which will unloose your vanity of Self
so that it spoils for you the spirit light'.
He also gave this solemn warning:
'In silent hours of your devotion search
how this delusion as soul fiend
imperils the spirit seeker's path.
He who falls prey to it may see
our human nature in those spheres where
   only spirit
reveals itself to spirit light.
If you would worthily prepare yourselves
to take in with your eye of soul
the light of wisdom streaming from the
   Christ,
you must keep careful watch upon
   yourselves

that self-delusion may not blind you
in moments when you think it far
    removed'.
By keeping these words well in mind
we'll soon give up the false idea
that we can easily today hand over
the teachings that our souls profess.
We must take comfort from the fact
that we encounter many a soul
who in our day unconsciously receives
the seed for future lives on earth.
This seed may seem at first
in conflict with those powers
to which in later times it will submit itself.
Within that hatred which pursues us now
I can find only seeds of future love.

FIRST MASTER OF CEREMONY

It's certain that the goal of highest truth
can be revealed in words like these.
Yet it seems hard already in these times
to guide our lives according to their
    wisdom.

SECOND MASTER OF CEREMONY

Here, too, I can accept our masters' words:
'It is not granted to all men
to live earth's future in advance.
But such men always must be found
who can foresee the shape of later days.
They'll dedicate their heart to forces

that can release existence from the present
and guard it safely for eternity'.

SCENE NINE

(The peasants in a forest glade)

FIFTH WOMAN   I've said it time and time again:
their lordship's rule must vanish.
Indeed a dream has shown to me
how we can serve the troops
and care for them right well
when they arrive to carry out the siege.

SIXTH PEASANT   If dreams are still to be believed,
we do not need to question.
The knights have tried to
make us more intelligent
than were our fathers,
and now they shall find out
just how much cleverer we have become.
Our fathers gave them welcome here,
but we will chase them out.
I know the secret passageways
which lead into the castle.
I used to work up there
until my anger drove me out.
I'll show the noble knights
how science can be useful.

FOURTH WOMAN   He's surely planning nothing good,
               I feel quite frightened at his words.

FIFTH PEASANT   I have been shown already in a vision
                how soon by secret ways a traitor
                will lead the enemy into the castle.

SIXTH WOMAN   I find such visions most pernicious.
              If we can think as Christians still,
              then we should know that honesty,
              not treachery, will rescue us from evil.

              . . .

Notes

There are many worthwhile 'conventional' histories of the Order, such as Edith Simon: *The Piebald Standard,* Cassell 1959, or more recently Piers Paul Read: *The Templars,* Phoenix Press 1999, or the work of Malcolm Barber, see below.

Notes 55–65 are by Hella Wiesberger from *The Temple Legend* (Rudolf Steiner Press, 1997), pp. 359–365. The source for the lecture text to which they relate is shorthand notes by Walter Vegelahn and Berta Reebstein-Lehmann, and longhand notes by Marie Steiner von Sievers.

1. J. M. Upton-Ward, *The Rule of the Templars* (London: The Boydell Press, 1992).
2. Virginia Sease and Manfred Schmidt-Brabant, *Paths of the Christian Mysteries* (London: Temple Lodge, 2003).
2a. As above, also Jacques de Mahieu, *Les Templiers en Amérique* (Paris: Editions Robert Laffont, 1981).
3. Malcolm Barber, *The Trial of the Templars* (Cambridge University Press, 1978).
4. Rudolf Steiner, *Inner Impulses of Evolution: the Mexican Mysteries and the Knights Templar,* lecture of 25 September 1916 (GA 171) revised by G. Church (New York: Anthroposophic Press, 1984).
5. Rudolf Steiner, lecture 2 October 1916 (GA 171). See Lecture 4 in this volume.

6. See for instance in several lectures in *The Christian Mystery* (GA 97) (Lower Beachmont, Australia: Completion Press, 2000).

6a. The Manichaeans were a branch of Christianity founded by Mani in the third century and were preoccupied with the problem of evil. Steiner describes them as preparing for a future transformation of evil. As a result they tried to lead very pure lives. They came to look upon matter as created by darkness or evil which must be overcome by light or goodness and which unites with it for that purpose. This earned them the name of *dualist*, and their beliefs led in later centuries to so-called heretical sects such the Paulicians, the Bogomils or Bulgars and the Cathars.

7. Rudolf Steiner, undated typescript translation from *Gäa Sophia*, Vol. III, 'The Migration of Races', Z 345. (See 3 in Sources.)

8. Wolfram's use of the unfamiliar word *Templiesen* has caused some commentators to deny this connection, but one explanation is that he was using, as he did with many of the names, a kind of translation from the Provençal.

9. See note 4.

10. Rudolf Steiner: *Concerning the History and Content of the Higher Degrees of the Esoteric School 1904–1914* (GA 265); tr. John Wood (Switzerland and Isle of Mull: Etheric Dimensions Press, 2005).

11. Rudolf Steiner, *The Temple Legend*, lecture 22 May 1905 'Concerning the Lost Temple and How it is to be Restored' (GA 93) tr. John Wood (London: Rudolf Steiner Press, 1997).

12. See note 4.

13. Rudolf Steiner, *The Book of Revelation* (GA 346) lecture 12

September 1924, tr. J. Collis (London: Rudolf Steiner Press, 1998).

13a. The name given to one of the powers opposing good, taken from the ancient Persian belief.

14. Gérard Serbanesco, *Histoire de L'Ordre des Templiers et les Croisades* (Paris: Les Editions Byblos, 1969).

15. A. Bothwell-Gosse, *The Knights Templars* (London: The Office of the Co-Mason, n.d.).

16. Pope Nicholas I, Pope from 858–867, intelligent and uncompromising, upheld the Papacy against worldly princes and church dignitaries.

17. T.H. Meyer, ed. *Light for the New Millenium: Rudolf Steiner's association with Helmuth and Eliza von Moltke*, tr. H. Herrmann-Davey, W. Forward and M. Askew (London: Rudolf Steiner Press, 1997).

18. Knights of St John, the Knights Hospitaller. Founded around 1100 to care for sick pilgrims in Jerusalem. Moved to Cyprus in 1291, to Rhodes in 1309 and to Malta in 1530 where they became the Knights of Malta.

19. Peter of Amiens, c.1050–1115, a pilgrim preacher who collected a large following of peasants and townsfolk in France. They travelled to Jerusalem but many were killed in Hungary and in the Near East.

20. Godfrey of Bouillon, c.1060–1100, Burgundian knight who led the crusade to capture Jerusalem for the Christians in 1099, brother to Baldwin, the first king of Jerusalem.

21. St Bernard of Clairvaux, 1090–1153, Cistercian leader who preached the call to the second Crusade in 1147.

22. Titurel, said to be the first Grail King.

23. Parsifal: Chrétien de Troyes, *Perceval*, c.1180; Wolfram von Eschenbach, *Parzival*, c.1200.

24. Boniface, c.680–754. Scottish Benedictine monk who became archbishop in the Frankish church. He acted in opposition to the Celtic Christian stream.

25. Grail and Arthurian streams—see *Karmic Relationships* (GA 240) Vol. VIII, lectures given in Torquay and London, August 1924 (London: Rudolf Steiner Press, 1975).

26. Realism and Nominalism. See *Human and Cosmic Thought* (GA 151) Berlin 21 January 1914 (London: Rudolf Steiner Press, 1991).

27. *Parsifal and Lohengrin,* Cologne, 3 December 1905 (GA 92) T/S Z 212.

28. Dionysius the Areopagite, converted by St Paul in Athens and founder of a Christian mystery school.

29. John Scotus Erigena, 810–877, an Irish monk who led the palace school of Charles the Bald, 828–877, in France.

30. *Secret Brotherhoods and the Mystery of the Human Double* (GA 178) St Gallen, Zurich and Dornach, between 6 and 25 November 1917 (London: Rudolf Steiner Press, 2004).

31. Goethe, *The Fairy Tale of the Green Snake and the Beautiful Lily,* tr. Thomas Carlyle (Stroud: Hawthorn Press, 1998).

32. Rudolf Steiner, *Four Mystery Dramas* (GA 14) tr. Hans and Ruth Pusch (London: Rudolf Steiner Press, 1997).

33. Five French knights? Historical accounts usually state nine.

34. Boniface VIII, Pope from 1294–1303. He was brutally taken prisoner by Philip the Fair's counsellor William of Nogaret. Although freed after three days, he died, probably of shock, after a few weeks.

35. Clement V, Pope from 1305–1314.

36. Mexican Mysteries. See previous lecture in *The Inner Impulses of Evolution* (note 4 above).

36a. A performance of *Faust* had presumably just taken place.

37. Julius Mosen, 1803–1867, 'Ahasver' 1838, 'Ritter Wahn' 1831.

38. *Aus dem mitteleuropäischen Geistesleben*, Berlin, 15 April 1916 (GA 65) not translated.

39. George Henry Lewes, *The Life and Works of Goethe* (London: Smith, Elder, 1855).

40. Alexander Baumgartner S.J., *Goethe*, 1885–86.

41. Ralph Waldo Emerson, 1803–1882. *Essays 1841–46*, *Representative Men*, 1850 (London: Routledge, 1889).

42. Goethe, 'The Mysteries', a poem (Spring Valley, N.Y: Mercury Press, 1987). Translator unknown.

43. Anastasius Grün (Anton Alexander Graf von Auersperg), 1806–1876, *Schutt*, 1835.

43a. 5 May 1912, (GA 130), *The Festivals and their Meaning* (GA various) (London: Rudolf Steiner Press, 1996).

44. 'Passage I read years ago' ... see lecture 2 May 1912, Berlin, *Earthly and Cosmic Man* (GA 133) (Blauvelt: Garber Communications, 1986).

45. See note13a. Goethe used the name Mephistopheles for this being.

46. Rudolf Steiner seems to be hinting at what he called 'eugenic occultism', see lecture 1 December 1918, *The Challenge of the Times* (GA 186) (New York: Anthroposophic Press, 1941).

47. The stage of earth evolution which preceded Atlantis, see *Occult Science / An Outline of Esoteric Science* (GA 13) (London: R. Steiner Press, 1984 / New York: Anthroposophic Press, 1997).

48. Luigi Galvani 1737–1798, Italian physiologist who discovered animal electricity.
Alessandro Volta 1745–1827, Italian physicist, inventor of the electric battery.

49. *Three Streams in the Evolution of Mankind* (GA 184) Dornach 4–13 October 1918 (London: Rudolf Steiner Press, 1965).

50. The Hebrew characters with their numerical equivalents are shown here in the traditional sequence. (See R. Steiner *The Apocalypse of St John. Lectures on the Book of Revelation* (GA 104), tr. rev. J. Collis (London: Rudolf Steiner Press, 1977). See the special note on p. 263 of R. Steiner *Die Apokalypse des Johannes* (GA 104) (Dornach: Verlag am Goetheanum, 1985). It is not known why Rudolf Steiner used the spelling Soradt (Notebook entry, Archive No. 498). Another representation of the number 666 is found in Agrippa von Nettesheim's *De occulta philosophia*, Part II, Chapter 22:

Magic Square of the Sun

in

Numbers.   Hebrew Characters.

6	32	3	34	35	1
7	11	27	28	8	30
19	14	16	15	23	24
18	20	22	21	17	13
25	29	10	9	26	12
36	5	33	4	2	31

ו	לב	ג	לד	לה	א
ז	יא	כז	כח	ח	ל
יט	יד	יו	יה	כג	כד
יח	כ	כב	כא	יז	יג
כה	כט	י	ט	כו	יב
לו	ה	לג	ד	ב	לא

'... The fourth magic square, that of the sun, consists of the square of six and contains thirty-six numbers, six in each row, and diagonally from corner to corner, each row having the sum of one hundred and eleven. The sum of all the numbers is six hundred and sixty-six'.

Regarding Sorat and 666, see also 27 April 1907 (GA 96) *Original Impulses for the Science of the Spirit* (Lower Beachmont, Australia: Completion Press, 2001).

51. See 10 September 1924, *Karmic Relationships*, Vol. IV (GA

238) tr. G. Adams, rev. D.S. Osmond, C. Davy (London: Rudolf Steiner Press, 1997).

52. *Concerning the History and Content of the Higher Degrees of the Esoteric School, 1904–1914* (GA 265) tr. John Wood (Switzerland and Isle of Mull: The Etheric Dimensions Press, 2005).

53. Lynn Picknett and Clive Prince, *The Sion Revelation* (New York: Simon and Schuster, 2006).

54. Virginia Sease and Manfred Schmidt-Brabant: *Denker, Heilige, Ketzer* (Dornach: Verlag am Goetheanum, 2005). Forthcoming English edition to be published by Temple Lodge.

55. I Kings 5–7.
II Chronicles 3–4.
Ezekiel 40–42.

56. Jean Paul (pseudonym for Jean Paul Friedrich Richter), 1763–1825, poet, writer of novels, and thinker. The episode here related was recorded in his childhood reminiscences.

57. This took place once a year on the Day of Atonement. Leviticus 16:29–34: 'And this shall be an everlasting statute unto you, to make an atonement for the children of Israel, for all their sins, once a year'.

58. According to notes of a lecture by Rudolf Steiner given in Cologne on 28 December 1907 (GA 101, not published in English) he states:

> Were we to take millennia into account rather than centuries, we would observe how the form of the human body undergoes change according to the thoughts, feelings and conceptual criteria of previous millennia; and the mighty leading powers of evolution give to

human beings the right concepts at the right time, so that even the human form becomes transformed . . .

How did the whole length, width and height of the physical body of today actually evolve? It is a result of what was at first contained in the astral and etheric bodies. That was where the thoughts, pictures, feelings, etc., at first resided. You will better be able to understand what I have to say if you call to mind a process which takes place immediately after physical death. It happens then that the physical body is at first abandoned by the etheric and astral bodies. Sleep consists of the fact that the astral body and ego withdraw leaving the physical body and etheric body lying in bed. Death is differentiated from sleep through the fact that in the former state the physical body alone remains behind on the bed and the etheric body withdraws along with the other two members of the human being. A strange phenomenon then takes place which could be described as a sensation but which is connected with a kind of concept. The person feels as if he were expanding and then the memory tableau occurs; but before that happens he feels himself expanding in all directions—he gains in dimension on all sides.

This view of his etheric body in huge dimensions is a very important concept; for it had to be induced into Atlantean human beings at a time when their etheric body was not so closely knit with the physical body as it was to be in post-Atlantean times. This concept, which occurs in human beings at death today, had first to be awoken in them at that time. If a person were to visualize the approximate dimensions which are experienced by the human being today when he expands at death, then he has created the pattern, the thought form, which is able to bring his physical body into approximately its present form. If, therefore, the true measurements were held up in front of a person whose etheric body was at times separated from his physical body, they would take on the form that the physical body has today. And this form would have been induced into the human being primarily by those who are leaders of humankind's development. The exact account of this is contained in the various stories of the flood, particularly the biblical account. If you were to visualize the human being more or less surrounded by those forms which the etheric body must have in order that the physical body can be built up according to its proper dimensions, then you would have the same dimensions as Noah's Ark.

Why are the exact measurements of Noah's Ark given in the Bible? So that a human being who was to be the bridge from Atlantean times to post-Atlantean times would have a structure 300 cubits long, 50 cubits broad, 30 cubits high, which he must have around him in order to build up the proper thought form, to develop the right pattern out of length, width and height, to build up the post-Atlantean body in the right way. There you have a symbol from which the dimensions of your present-day body have been taken and which are the result of the thought form which Noah experienced in the Ark. It is not for nothing that Noah was placed in the Ark and that the Ark was described in this way. The Ark was built thus so that the human body could be properly formed in post-Atlantean times. The whole of humankind was educated by means of the use of effective symbols. The human being carries with him in the present day the measurements of Noah's Ark. When the human being stretches his hands upwards the measurements of the Ark come to expression in the measurements of the human being's present-day body. Now the human being has evolved from Atlantis to post-Atlantis. In the epoch which will follow ours, the sixth epoch, the human being's body will again be quite differently formed; and today, too, the human being must experience those thought forms which will enable him to create for the next epoch the patterns to provide the proper measurements for the body. That must be presented to the human being. Today the measurements of the human being's body are in the proportion of 300 to 50 to 30. In the future his body will be built up quite differently. What will supply the present-day human being with the thought form for building up his future body? That is also told us. It is the measurements of Solomon's Temple. And these measurements of Solomon's Temple, when realized in physical form, represent with profound symbolical significance the whole physical organization of the human being of the next epoch, the sixth great epoch.

Everything which is effective in humankind has its beginning inside the human being, not outside. What appears as thought and feeling in one period is outward form in the next. And the individuals who guide humankind must implant the thought forms into the human being many thousands of years in advance if they are to become outward reality later. There you have the working of the thought forms which are activated by such symbolical figures. They have a very real meaning.

59.   It has not been possible to identify the literary source to which Rudolf Steiner here refers.

In the *Cabbala* of Agrippa von Nettesheim (Stuttgart: Scheible edition, 1855), it is stated in the chapter concerning 'The Measurement, Relationship and Harmony of the Human Body':

> Yes, God Himself instructed Noah in the building of the Ark according to the measurements of the human body, just as He Himself incorporated into the whole world mechanism the symmetry of the human being; and therefore the latter is called the macrocosm, the former the microcosm. With reference to the above, some microcosmologists determine the measurements of the human body as being six foot, the foot being ten degrees and the degree being five minutes; this amounts to 60 degrees or 300 minutes, the same number of geometrical cubits as, according to the description of Moses, were contained in the length of the Ark. Just as the human body, however, has a length of 300 minutes, a width of 50 and a thickness of 30, so had the Ark of Noah not only a length of 300 cubits, but also a width of 50 and a depth (or height) of 30, from which it will be seen that there is a relationship of 6 to 1 of the length to the breadth, 10 to 1 of the length to the depth and 5 to 3 of the width to the depth.

Further to this, Franz Coci in his work *Detailed Calculation of the Three Dimensions of Noah's Ark from the Standpoint of*

Geometry and Mechanics (translated from Polish into German by Wenzel Bauernöpl, Bilin, 1899), demonstrated mathematically that: 'The only fitting and possible relationship of width to height of a four-sided hollow body, which combines the use of the least amount of material with the greatest stability, would be to take 5 (more precisely 5.322232) equal parts for the width and 3 (more precisely 2.967768) for the height. And this is the ratio in which the Ark actually was built'.

60. The version here translated is the version from the notes of Berta Reebstein-Lehmann. Walter Vegelahn's version is only fragmentary. It is rendered thus: 'The . . . temple is so formed that it encloses the fivefold human being. That . . . is the most important thing about the temple. The square is holy, the roof, the roof-covering and the side pillars together form . . . In front of the altar stood two cherubim'.

61. I Kings 6:31: 'And for the entering of the oracle he made doors of olive tree: the lintel and side posts were a fifth part of the wall.' The gloss referring to 'fifth part' gives the alternative 'five-square'.

Emil Bock, speaking about the Temple of Solomon, says in his *Kings and Prophets*: 'The third, inmost chamber in the west, the Holy of Holies (Debir), was screened by a wooden partition containing a pentagonal doorway and covered by a curtain of four colours'.

62. The text is quite plainly only preserved in an incomplete form. In connection with the cultural epochs and the course of the sun through the zodiac, see Rudolf Steiner's lecture given in Dornach on 8 January 1918, in the lecture course entitled *Ancient Myths* (GA 180) (New York: Anthroposophic Press, 1994).

63. Rudolf Steiner often quotes this passage from Plato's *Timaeus*, but his formulation is closer to that of Vincenz Knauer, a Viennese philosopher personally known to him, whose book *Die Hauptprobleme der Philosophie* ... (*The Development and Partial Solution to the Main Philosophical Problems from the Time of Thaïes to Robert Hamerling*) formed part of his personal library. In this particular version the passage here quoted has the following wording: 'God laid this soul in cross-formation through the universe and spread out over it the world body'. In the English translation of this passage (Penguin Classics, 1971, p. 48) it reads as follows: 'He then took the whole fabric and cut it down the middle into two strips, which he placed crossways at their middle points to form a shape like the letter X; he then bent the ends round in a circle and fastened them to each other opposite the point at which the strips crossed, to make two circles, one inner and one outer'.

However, neither Plato's *Timaeus*, nor Vincenz Knauer's book in which he had underlined the pertinent passage, appears to be the source for the description used here. It seems rather that Rudolf Steiner has discovered in these philosophers something which put him on to the track of what he himself had found out, which would explain the deviation from the descriptions of both of these writers. This way of enlivening and verifying his spiritual revelations with historical records is described by him in his autobiography, *The Story of My Life* (London: Anthroposophical Pub., 1928) Chap. 26:

My relationship to Christianity should make it clear that my science of the spirit is not attained through research of the kind ascribed to me by many people. They intimate that I have put together a theory of the spirit on the basis of ancient traditions. I am supposed to have elaborated Gnosticism and other teachings. The spiritual insight gained in *Christianity as Mystical Fact* is brought directly out of the world of spirit. It was only because I wished to demonstrate to the audience at these lectures, and to the readers of the book, the harmony between what can be perceived in the spirit and the records of history, that I examined the latter and incorporated them in the content. But I took nothing from these documents unless I had first experienced it in the spirit.

64. This passage is very incomplete. In the Vegelahn text there are only the words as given above. In the text given by Reebstein it continues: 'But the Temple is not yet understood by human beings'. Perhaps the correct rendering should be: 'But the building of the Temple is not yet understood by human beings'.

65. In the Vegelahn text this sentence finds an incomplete continuation: 'These two streams already made themselves felt at the beginning of our race—the old stream which entered evolution at a time when the gods were still engaged in creating the world, and the second ... which must always continue to build in this Temple of Wisdom ...'.

66. Mechthild Werner: *Burgenland. Aus dem Lande in dem Rudolf Steiner seine Jugend verbrachte* (Dornach: Rudolf Geering Verlag, 1961).

67. Jacques de Molay.

68. The Brotherhood was encouraged to seek out the excommunicated.

Sources

1. Pope Nicholas I and the spiritual life of Europe
'Pope Nicholas I and the spiritual life of Europe', Dornach, 1 October 1922, tr. D.S.Osmond and Owen Barfield, in *Supersensible Influences in the History of Mankind* (GA 216) (London: Rudolf Steiner Publishing Co., 1956).

2. The Templars and the Church of Rome
Lecture, Berlin, 28 December 1904, in *Über Philosophophie, Geschichte und Literatur* (GA 51) (Dornach: Rudolf Steiner Verlag, 1983).

3. The Templars as initiates of the Grail
'On the Migration of the Races', ? Berlin 1904. T/S Z 345, 'Über die Wanderung der Rassen', *Gäa Sophia*, Vol. III (Stuttgart: Orient-Occident Verlag, 1929).

4. The Templars and the forces of evil
Lecture, Dornach, 25 September 1916, in *Inner Impulses of Evolution: The Mexican Mysteries and the Knights Templar* (GA 171), rev. by G.Church, F.Kozlik and S.C.Easton (New York: Anthroposophic Press, 1984).
Lecture, Dornach, 2 October 1916. Formerly T/S Z 156 (from GA 171).

5. Sorat and the demise of the Templars
Lecture, Dornach, 12 September 1924, in *The Book of Revelation and the Work of the Priest* (GA 346) tr. J. Collis (London: Rudolf Steiner Press, 1998).

6. Templar beliefs

Lecture, Berlin 22 May 1905, in 'Concerning the Lost Temple and How it is to be Restored II', *The Temple Legend and the Golden Legend* (GA 93) tr. John Wood (London: Rudolf Steiner Press, 1997).

7. The Soul's Probation (Four Mystery Plays)

Tr. Ruth and Hans Pusch (London: Rudolf Steiner Press, 1997).

Note on Rudolf Steiner's Lectures

The lectures and addresses contained in this volume have been translated from the German, which is based on stenographic and other recorded texts that were in most cases never seen or revised by the lecturer. Hence, due to human errors in hearing and transcription, they may contain mistakes and faulty passages. Every effort has been made to ensure that this is not the case. Some of the lectures were given to audiences more familiar with anthroposophy; these are the so-called 'private' or 'members' lectures. Other lectures, like the written works, were intended for the general public. The difference between these, as Rudolf Steiner indicates in his *Autobiography*, is twofold. On the one hand, the members' lectures take for granted a background in and commitment to anthroposophy; in the public lectures this was not the case. At the same time, the members' lectures address the concerns and dilemmas of the members, while the public work arises from, and directly addresses Steiner's own understanding of universal needs. Nevertheless, as Rudolf Steiner stresses: 'Nothing was ever said that was not solely the result of my direct experience of the growing content of anthroposophy. There was never any question of concessions to the prejudices and preferences of the members. Whoever reads these privately printed lectures can take them to represent anthroposophy in the fullest sense. Thus it was possible without hesitation—when the complaints in this direction became too persistent—to depart from the custom of circulating this material "For members only". But it must be borne in mind that faulty passages do occur in these reports not revised by myself.'

Earlier in the same chapter, he states: 'Had I been able to correct them [*the private lectures*], the restriction *for members only* would have been unnecessary from the beginning.' The original German editions on which this text is based were published by Rudolf Steiner Verlag, Dornach, Switzerland in the collected edition (*Gesamtausgabe*, 'GA') of Rudolf Steiner's work. All publications are edited by the Rudolf Steiner Nachlassverwaltung (estate), which wholly owns both Rudolf Steiner Verlag and the Rudolf Steiner Archive.

Rudolf Steiner
The Interior of the Earth
An Esoteric Study of the Subterranean Spheres

Modern science can speak with authority regarding only a tiniest fraction
of the earth's interior. We have, quite literally, scratched just the surface of
our planet. Can we truly know what lies beneath our feet, in the
unimaginably deep, hidden depths of the earth? Can the phenomenon of
spiritual investigation add to this question?

In this comprehensive volume, with notes and an introduction, Rudolf
Steiner's utterances on this theme have been brought together for the first
time under one cover. His unique overview gives a picture of the nine
layers of the earth as they become visible via the research of the spiritual
scientist. The layers range from the familiar 'mineral' on which we live, to
the innermost core which Steiner connects to human and animal powers of
reproduction. In between are layers such as the 'Mirror Earth', which
represents qualities of extreme evil, and the 'Fire Earth', which is
connected to natural catastrophes.

The information Steiner conveys is never abstract or theoretical, but
intimately related to the human being. The Fire Earth, for example, is
acutely affected by people's will. When the human will is chaotic and
untutored, says Steiner, it acts magnetically on this layer and disrupts it,
leading to volcanic eruptions. He also describes other natural
catastrophes—such as extreme weather and earthquakes—in connection
to the interior of the earth and karma.

In the final section Steiner explains the human being's role in relation to
both the celestial and subterranean spheres. The Appendix features
supplementary material in the shape of an essay on the theme by one of
Steiner's closest pupils, Adolf Arenson, and a remarkable memoir of
conversations with Steiner by Countess Johanna Keyserlingk.

Intro. P.V. O'Leary (*Selected lectures, various GAs*); 144pp;
21.5 × 13.5 cm; pb; 978 1 85584 119 2; £9.95

Rudolf Steiner
The Incarnation of Ahriman
The Embodiment of Evil on Earth

While we know of Ahriman from Persian mythology, Rudolf Steiner spoke of him as an actual, living spiritual entity. This being, he said, works to embed people firmly into physicality, encouraging dull, materialistic attitudes and a philistine, dry intellect. In these extraordinary lectures Steiner, in rare prophetic mode, talks about an actual incarnation of Ahriman on the earth and the potential consequences. Just as Christ incarnated in a physical body, so would Ahriman incarnate in the Western world—before 'a part' of the third millennium had passed.

Steiner places this incarnation in the context of a 'cosmic triad'—Lucifer, Christ and Ahriman. Ahriman will incarnate as a counterpoint to the physical incarnation of Lucifer in the East in the third millennium BC, with the incarnation of Jesus Christ in Palestine as the balancing point between the two.

Over the period during which Steiner developed anthroposophy—a speaking career that spanned two decades and more than six thousand lectures—he referred to the idea of Ahriman's incarnation only seven times. Six lectures, together with an additional supporting excerpt, are reproduced here in their entirety, and under one cover, for the first time.

Intro. S. Gulbekian (*7 lectures, various GAs*); 128pp; 21.5 × 13.5 cm; pb; 978 1 85584 178 9; £8.95

Rudolf Steiner
The Lord's Prayer
An Esoteric Study

The Lord's Prayer stands at the heart of Christianity. Over the past two millennia it has been spoken millions of times by millions of people around the world. Rudolf Steiner affirms the power of this prayer, given by Jesus Christ himself, and encourages us to begin to understand it at deeper levels. Such an understanding, he explains, is now necessary for humanity's further development.

In the four lectures he gave on this subject, collected here under one cover, Rudolf Steiner penetrates the esoteric meanings of the Lord's Prayer, relating its seven petitions to the seven spiritual and physical bodies of the human being. He also discusses the difference between prayer and meditation, and shows how true prayer is selfless in nature.

This volume features an introduction by Judith von Halle, whose work is valued for her experiential knowledge of the Lord's Prayer and the events of Christ's life.

Intro. J. von Halle (*4 lectures from GAs 96 + 97*); 88pp; 21.5 × 13.5 cm; pb; ISBN 978 1 85584 164 2; £7.95